Giovanni Battista Pagani

Devotion to the Most Holy Sacrament

Giovanni Battista Pagani

Devotion to the Most Holy Sacrament

ISBN/EAN: 9783743383593

Manufactured in Europe, USA, Canada, Australia, Japa

Cover: Foto ©Lupo / pixelio.de

Manufactured and distributed by brebook publishing software (www.brebook.com)

Giovanni Battista Pagani

Devotion to the Most Holy Sacrament

DEVOTION

TO THE

Most Holy Sacrament

TRANSLATED FROM THE ITALIAN

OF

JOHN BAPTIST PAGANI

Author of "The Anima Divota"

A NEW AND REVISED EDITION

LONDON
Art and Book Company
AND LEAMINGTON
1892

TO

HIS BELOVED SISTERS IN CHRIST,

WHO HAVE CHOSEN THE BETTER PART,

THE SISTERS OF PROVIDENCE,

THIS LITTLE WORK

IS RESPECTFULLY INSCRIBED

BY THE AUTHOR.

PREFACE TO THE SECOND EDITION.

A LEARNED prelate, writing on the names given in the Church's Liturgy to the Holy Eucharist, very properly says that each name is a *picture*. In like manner, we might say that a well-chosen sentence from the Holy Scriptures is a *Treatise*, for it supplies abundant matter for reflection according to each one's own disposition and devotion.

This we consider to be the special merit of the little book of which we offer to the public a second edition.

The writer of the *Devotion to the Blessed Sacrament*, the pious author of *The Anima Divota*, furnishes the Devout Soul with many well-chosen passages from Holy Writ for each day of the month, having reference to Our Lord Jesus Christ in the Blessed Sacrament. Each visit dwells on one of the many aspects in which we may contemplate Our Lord in the Sacrament of His love. The texts of Scripture, chiefly selected from the New Testament, which are prefixed to the divisions of each Visit, supply matter of thought and devout affections to the pious worshipper.

This edition, carefully revised, is a faithful translation of the original Italian work, which was first printed in Milan in 1845, and has since passed through many editions.

D. G.

CONTENTS.

		PAGE
On the practice of Visiting the most Holy Sacrament		1
On Spiritual Communion		4
Acts which should be made at the beginning of each Visit to the most Holy Sacrament		7
Visit I.	Jesus our God,	8
Visit II.	Jesus our Creator,	11
Visit III.	Jesus our Preserver,	14
Visit IV.	Jesus our Saviour,	18
Visit V.	Jesus our Mediator,	21
Visit VI.	Jesus our Head,	26
Visit VII.	Jesus our Master,	30
Visit VIII.	Jesus our King,	34
Visit IX.	Jesus our Legislator,	38
Visit X.	Jesus our True Lover,	42
Visit XI.	Jesus our Benefactor,	47
Visit XII.	Jesus our Father,	52
Visit XIII.	Jesus our Brother,	58
Visit XIV.	Jesus our Friend,	63
Visit XV.	Jesus our Spouse,	69
Visit XVI.	Jesus our Teacher,	73
Visit XVII.	Jesus our Leader,	78
Visit XVIII.	Jesus our Physician,	82
Visit XIX.	Jesus our Shepherd,	86
Visit XX.	Jesus our Advocate,	90

CONTENTS.

Visit XXI.	Jesus our High Priest,	94
Visit XXII.	Jesus our Guest,	98
Visit XXIII.	Jesus our Pattern,	102
Visit XXIV.	Jesus our Food,	106
Visit XXV.	Jesus our Life,	111
Visit XXVI.	Jesus our Comforter,	115
Visit XXVII.	Jesus our Sanctifier,	119
Visit XXVIII.	Jesus our Judge,	124
Visit XXIX.	Jesus our Glorifier,	129
Visit XXX.	Jesus our All,	135
Visit XXXI.	Jesus our Victim,	140
Offerings of the Most Precious Blood of Jesus		146

DEVOTION

TO THE

MOST HOLY SACRAMENT.

—:o:—

On the Practice of Visiting the Most Holy Sacrament.

Our Lord Jesus Christ was not satisfied to remain with us only during the adorable sacrifice of the Mass, but He was pleased to make our altars His perpetual dwelling-place, that so He might be always ready to receive our visits, and to enrich us with His favours. Oh, what then should be our joy, what our confidence and heart-felt love, since we know that within our churches, and near to our homes, Jesus abides in the Blessed Sacrament, and abides there that He may bestow His graces upon us! What ought not to be our gratitude towards our most loving Jesus for that unspeakable goodness which has led Him to make His abode amongst us, that He may draw us to His sacred presence, and intimately unite Himself to our souls! What should be our care to visit Him often in this Divine Sacrament, and humbly to offer Him the homage of our adoration!

The saints, who loved Jesus Christ in very deed, found all their happiness in visiting Him frequently.

St. Vincent of Paul used to visit the Blessed Sacrament as often as he could during the day, and it was the greatest relief in the midst of his most pressing labours to spend a long time in prayer before the sacred Tabernacle; there would he kneel with a demeanour so humble, so modest, so devout, that he seemed to behold, even with the eyes of the body, the adorable person of Jesus Christ. Whenever he had any difficult business on hand, he would betake himself, like another Moses, to the sacred Tabernacle, there to consult the oracle of truth. Whenever he left the house, he would go first to ask a blessing from our Lord, and on his return would go at once to give thanks for all blessings received, and humbly to ask pardon for any fault he might have committed. St. Aloysius Gonzaga was full of joy whenever he could pass some time with his most dear Jesus, nor could he leave His presence without pain. St. Francis Xavier, in the midst of his incredible labours, found nothing that gave him so much relief as to pass a great part of the night before the most Holy Sacrament. St. Francis Regis used to do the same; and once, when he found the church closed, he remained outside the doors on his knees, exposed to the rain and cold, that he might, even at a distance, enjoy the company of his beloved Lord in the Blessed Sacrament.

Oh, what a boundless field for devotion is the altar where Jesus dwells in the Sacrament of His love! Right well was this understood by that blessed soul who, being asked why she remained so many hours before the Blessed Sacrament, replied: "Is there not present therein the very essence of God, Who is the food of the blessed, of that God who ravishes with ecstasies of love the holy Seraphim? What can the soul do before Jesus in the Blessed Sacrament but love, praise, give thanks and pray? What does a poor beggar do in the presence of a rich and powerful lord? a sick man before his physician? one parched with thirst at a fountain of flowing water? one that is hungry at a plentiful table? Oh, I could remain there for ever!"

On Spiritual Communion.

Spiritual communion, a practice earnestly recommended at every visit to the Blessed Sacrament, consists, according to St. Thomas, in an ardent desire of receiving Jesus Christ, and in welcoming Him with loving embrace, as though we received Him sacramentally. This exercise devoutly practised has an especial efficacy for inflaming us more and more with the fire of divine love, and uniting us ever more closely with Christ our Lord.

The fittest time for making spiritual communion is during the holy Mass, and when we visit our Lord Jesus in the Blessed Sacrament. "Whenever you hear Mass," says St. Teresa, "endeavour also to make a spiritual communion, and from this you will gain the greatest spiritual profit." The faithful who assist at the holy sacrifice offer, along with the priest, before the throne of grace, not only prayers and praises, but the sacred Victim also; and Holy Church desires that all the faithful assisting at the sacrifice should partake together with the priest of the most holy Body of Jesus Christ. We find the holy Fathers most bitterly regretting the time when, the piety of Christians waxing cold, they began to give up the saintly custom of communicating daily at the Mass. The prayers recited by the priest in preparation and thanksgiving after holy communion are equally adapted to the use of the faithful assisting at Mass. These and similar reasons show most clearly that, if the faithful who are present at Mass cannot communicate sacramentally, they ought at least to endeavour to communicate spiritually, that is, in heart and will.

Christians should also make a spiritual communion when they visit the most Holy Sacrament. The principal motive for which Jesus vouchsafes to remain amongst us in the Blessed Sacrament is to communicate Himself to our souls. So great a condescension on the part of our Lord requires our co-operation. But how can we respond to such an admirable invention of love, except by an ardent longing to be united to Him, and to receive Him into our heart at least when we find ourselves in His sacred presence?

In order, then, that you, O devout soul, may be well disposed for this holy exercise, begin by making an act of sincere contrition for all your sins, thus, as it were, to remove the dust from that chamber into which you desire your Lord to enter. Having done this, next excite yourself to a lively faith in the presence of Jesus Christ in this Divine Sacrament.

Consider briefly the grandeur and majesty of that God whom you behold hidden beneath the Eucharistic veil; ponder on the strength of that love and that infinite goodness which leads Him to desire earnestly to be united with so unworthy a creature; break forth into accents of humility and longing desire;—of humility, when you look upon your own unworthiness; of desire, when you behold the infinite bounty of your Lord. Seeing, then, that you cannot now unite yourself to Him really by sacramental communion, join yourself to Him at least in heart and affection, and say to Him in words of burning love: "Come, my dearest Jesus, come into this poor heart of mine; come and satiate my desires, come and sanctify my soul; come, my most sweet Jesus, come to my bosom." Imagine, then, that Mary, our most holy Mother, or some other of your patron saints, presents to you the sacred particle, receive Him from their hands, clasp Him to your bosom, press Him to your heart; after which, breaking forth in accents of thanksgiving and praise, beseech Him to bestow upon you those graces of which you find yourself most in need. You will thus, besides the present advantage which you draw from the spiritual communion, be most happily disposed to receive with increased devotion the real Body of your adorable

Redeemer when you approach the Eucharistic table. For, as wood which is kept warm and near the fire is the better prepared for burning, so a heart which is constantly kept warm with love towards Jesus in the Blessed Sacrament is easily caught by the sacred flame of love, when it approaches to that furnace of charity ever burning in these divine mysteries.

Acts

Which should be made at the beginning of each visit to the Most Holy Sacrament.

O devout soul, in order worthily to visit Jesus in the Blessed Sacrament, place yourself in His presence by an act of the most lively faith in your Lord concealed in the adorable Sacrament, of profound veneration, confidence, and love towards His sacred person.

Ask, in the next place, the grace to spend holily the time you pass in His presence.

And, lastly, unite yourself in spirit with the angels, who, prostrate before the sacred altar, offer up their never ceasing adorations to the immaculate Lamb.

Visit I.

In which we contemplate Jesus in the Blessed Sacrament as our God.

I. "*Thou art Christ, the Son of the living God.*"* One of the principal glories God vouchsafed to the Israelites of old was that they were often visited by the angel of the Lord. But how far higher is our glory, in that we have with us perpetually in the most Holy Sacrament, not a Cherub or a Seraph, but the Son of the living God Himself! Humble though the outward appearances in which He reveals Himself in this Divine Sacrament, yet is He certainly present who is the only begotten of the Father, the brightness of His glory, the image of His substance, and the infinitely worthy object of His complacency. As it was love which led Him to hide His divine majesty beneath the form of an infant at Bethlehem, and under the semblance of a malefactor on the cross, so here, in this Divine Sacrament, He hides the glory of His divinity beneath the semblance of bread, in order to communicate Himself to our souls. Oh, most admirable invention of love! Who will not love a God so infinitely lovely?

II. "*Neither is there any nation so great*

---
* Matt. xvi. 16.

that hath gods so nigh them, as our God is present to all our petitions." * What people on the face of the earth in their wildest dreams ever imagined their gods so near to them as our true God is to us? Who would have imagined it possible that the God of majesty and of glory, to show His love towards us, would deign to dwell perpetually in our churches, and close to our very habitations; that He would place His delight in admitting us at all times to His presence, and in conversing with us? Oh, prodigy of love! Oh, infinite abyss of charity!

III. "*Thou shalt love the Lord thy God with thy whole heart, and with thy whole soul, and with thy whole mind.*" † Behold, O devout soul, what your Lord requires from you. Far from driving you from His presence, as your sins have deserved, He calls upon you to love Him without reserve, and with all your powers. Oh, do you not marvel at this infinite condescension of your God, who deigns to admit you to such an honour? Is it not the height of glory to be able to love a God of infinite bounty—that God, a single ray of whose countenance ravishes with ecstasies of adoring wonder the whole multitude of the blessed spirits in heaven, and forms the very delight of Paradise? But how have you hitherto

---

* Deut. iv. 7.   † Matt. xxii. 37.

corresponded to so great a grace? how have you met His loving invitations? how have you obeyed His commands?

Ah, woe is me, that, instead of loving so good a God, I have shamefully turned my back upon Him, and have offended in a thousand ways this infinite majesty! Alas, have pity, my most sweet Jesus, have pity on this miserable sinner! "God be merciful to me a sinner."* Do not treat me according to my merits, but according to the multitude of Thy mercies. Fill my heart, O Lord, with a lively sorrow for my sins, and give me grace henceforth to consecrate myself wholly to Thy love. And whom shall I love if I love not Thee, O majesty and bounty infinite? O dearest Jesus, I do desire to love Thee; I desire to consecrate my whole heart to Thy love. What are pleasures to me? what are riches? what are honours? O my God, I care for nothing in the world but Thee. O my most sweet Lord, "Thou art the God of my heart, and my portion for ever." †

Pray for me, Mary my sweetest Mother, obtain that my heart may evermore melt with tenderness of love towards thy Divine Son.

EJACULATION.—Have mercy, O my God, on this miserable sinner.

(Finish the visit with a spiritual communion.)

---

* Luke xvii. 13. † Psalm lxxii. 26.

Visit II.

In which we contemplate Jesus in the Blessed Sacrament as our Creator.

I. "*The Word was God......all things were made by Him.*" * Who was it, O devout soul, that gave you being and life, together with all those gifts of nature and of grace with which you are adorned? Ah, you know full well who is the author of these excellent gifts. It is Jesus, that same Jesus who is enclosed within yonder sacred Tabernacle, and from thence regards you with eyes of the most loving tenderness. He is your Creator; and all that you are, and all that you possess, comes to you from His hand, and is the gracious gift of His bounty. "He made us, and not we ourselves." † He it was who gave you your natural life, when He drew you out of nothing, and breathed into your body the breath of life. He has, moreover, given you the supernatural life of grace, enlightening your mind with the light of faith, and kindling in your heart the fire of His holy love. Ah, then, does not so good a Lord deserve all your gratitude? And have you, then, the courage to offend Him? Is it possible that

---
* John i.   † Psalm xcix. 3.

you have dared to abuse His graces, and to turn His gifts against the Giver?

II. "*And every one that calleth upon My name, I have created him for My glory. I have formed him, and made him.*" * See, O devout soul, the end for which our most loving Jesus has drawn us out of nothing, and has made us what we are. He has not created us that we may enjoy the false pleasures of this earth, and give our love to creatures, but that we may direct all our powers to love Him with our whole heart, and, doing in all things His holy will, come to glorify Him for ever in heaven, there, together with the angels and saints, to hymn His praises and be for ever absorbed in the ocean of His love. Behold the desire of the sweetest heart of Jesus. Behold that which moved him to breathe into our face the breath of life, and to give us a living soul.† What is there that we ought not to do to gain so exalted an end?

III. "*Remember thy Creator......before the sun and the light and the moon and the stars be darkened.*" ‡ What use, O devout soul, have you hitherto made of your life and of the other gifts which you have received from your Creator? How have you employed the

---

* Isaias xliii. 7.   † Gen. ii. 7.
‡ Eccles. xii. 1, 2.

powers of your body and the faculties of your mind? Have you kept your heart with all diligence? Have you consecrated it wholly to Him who has given it to you, and who claims it for His own? But, whatever has been your life in time past, at least, do not for the future forget your Creator. Remember Him while yet the day blesses you with its light, and before the dark night shall overtake you, that night in which no man can work. *

Ah, yes, my sweetest Lord, I wish evermore to have Thee in my thoughts, to bear Thee deeply graven on my heart. I thank Thee for having created me, and for having lavished numberless gifts upon me. O my dear Lord, I desire to live only for Thee. Grant that henceforth my every thought, my every sigh, my every breath, may tend to Thy glory and Thy love. "Create in me a clean heart, O God, and renew a right spirit within me." † Yes, dearest Jesus, take away from me this heart of stone, and give me a heart of flesh, that I may walk faithfully in the way of Thy commandments; oh, despise not the work of Thy own hands. "I am thine, oh, save me!" ‡

To you, my Mother, sweetest Mary, I commend myself. I hope for everything through your intercession.

---

* John ix. 4.   † Psalm l. 12.   ‡ Psalm cxviii. 94.

EJACULATION.—Jesus, my Creator, have mercy on me, and save my soul.

Visit III.

In which we contemplate Jesus in the Blessed Sacrament as our Preserver.

I. "*In Him we live and move and are.*"* What would have become of us, O devout soul, if our Lord and Creator had at any moment withdrawn His bountiful hand, and left us to ourselves and to our own weakness? That very instant, without doubt, we should have returned to that nothing from which we were first drawn by an act of His bounty. As the light would no longer diffuse itself over this universe, if the sun should cease to pour forth its rays, so, if the Divine Sun should cease to diffuse in our souls the light of life, we, too, should cease to exist, and should sink that instant into the nothingness from which we originally came. See here, then, O devout soul, a new motive which should bind thee to this thy most loving Jesus, who is present in the Divine Sacrament. It is true, we see not how He exerts over us His infinite power; but it is not less certain that we are always

---
* Acts xvii. 28.

in His hands, and that He ceases not to breathe into our frame the breath of life. As by His omnipotence He has called us out of nothing, so by the same omnipotence does He continually preserve our life, and thus in a manner sustain in our behalf the act of creation, so that, whether we live, or move, or breathe, all comes from Him—from the power of that omnipotent arm which upholds us. How, then, can we ever be ungrateful to a God of such infinite bounty?

II. "*As the living Father hath sent Me, and I live by the Father, so he that eateth Me the same also shall live by Me.*"* The bounty of Jesus Christ towards us is shown not only in preserving our natural life, but yet more gloriously in preserving the supernatural life of the soul by grace. For why is it that He dwells with us in this Sacrament of love? Why does He unite Himself with us, and communicate Himself to our souls? Behold the wonder of His bounty! He humbles Himself to this degree that He may nourish us with His own flesh, and that by His life we may live. "I am the Bread of Life," He says; "as the living Father hath sent Me, and I live by the Father, so he that eateth Me the same also shall live by Me." Hence the

---

* John vi. 58.

saints call this heavenly Sacrament the tree of life, the food of immortality.

III. "*Why will you die, O house of Israel?*" * As once the Lord deplored the blindness of His people of old when they turned their backs upon Him, so now, as He remains hidden beneath the sacramental species, does He with greater reason deplore the blindness of so many Christians, who, although they know that in Him they possess a never-failing fountain of life, yet ungratefully turn from Him, and bring upon themselves a deplorable death. "Ah, unfortunate beings," does He exclaim from the Sacred Tabernacle, "why will you not come to My bosom, that you may partake of the water of salvation springing up unto life eternal? Do you not know that I have come to cast fire from heaven upon the earth, and that I long for nothing so much as that it be enkindled in your hearts? Know you not that the food which I dispense from this sacred place is the Bread of Life, whose property it is to restore and vivify the souls of men? Why, then, will you keep afar from Me, and cast yourselves into the arms of death? 'Why will you die, O house of Israel?'" What, O devout soul, shall we answer to these just complaints of our most loving Jesus?

* Ezech. xviii. 31.

Alas, have pity, O sweetest Jesus, on this miserable creature! It is, indeed, but too true that I have in times past been so ungrateful to Thee, and so cruel towards my own soul, as to turn my back upon Thy mercy to live after my own will and pleasure. It is but too true that I have chosen darkness rather than light, and death in preference to life. But henceforth I earnestly desire to be Thine, and Thine only. What will it profit me to gain the whole world, and to enjoy all its pleasures, if I lose Thee? Oh, permit me not at any time to be of the number of those wretched beings who walk in darkness and in the shadow of death. Draw me to Thee, O Lord, by the sweet chains of Thy grace, that I may worthily partake of Thy most sacred Body, and visit Thee with ardent devotion, as Thou dost remain in Thy most holy Tabernacle, that I may evermore be united with Thee, and that by Thy life I too may live. O my God, I look for this grace from Thy infinite bounty, and from thy intercession, O Mary, my sweetest Mother.

EJACULATION.—Preserve me, O Lord, from eternal death.

Visit IV.

In which we contemplate Jesus in the Blessed Sacrament as our Saviour.

I. "*Thou shalt call His name Jesus: for He shall save His people from their sins.*" * Words fail to express the depth of misery in which our poor humanity was sunk before the coming of Jesus Christ. Stripped of supernatural good and oppressed by innumerable evils, it groaned under the tyrannical sway of the powers of darkness, who aimed at its destruction. A poor wretch covered with ulcers from head to foot, a prisoner loaded with heavy fetters, are but faint images of man's lamentable condition. But who was it that drew him out of his hopeless misery? Who freed him from this horrible dungeon? Who rescued him from the jaws of eternal death? Lift up your eyes, O devout soul, and fix them on yonder sacred Tabernacle, for there you behold your liberator. It was Jesus who did this, that same Jesus who is now seated on our altars as on so many thrones of love. He it was who succoured us in our piteous case, and drew us forth from the profound abyss of wretchedness into which we

---

* Matt. i. 21.

had sunk. Clothed with our frail mortality, He appeared amongst men, not to judge and condemn the world, though its crimes called aloud for vengeance, but that through Him it might be saved. "For God sent not His Son into the world to judge the world, but that the world may be saved by Him."* Oh, tenderness! Oh, bounty unspeakable!

II. "*You were not redeemed with corruptible things, as gold and silver......but with the precious Blood of Christ, as of a lamb unspotted and undefiled.*" † What price did our most loving Jesus pay to ransom us from the slavery of hell, and place us in the way of salvation? Did He lavish gold or silver, or costliest gems? Be astounded, ye heavens, and you, O highest Seraphim, veil your faces in adoring wonder. The Son of the most high God paid our ransom with His own Blood—with that most precious Blood every drop of which was of infinite value. Ah, here indeed the powers of thought are confounded, and the mind is lost in an abyss of unfathomable mystery!

III. "*Blessed be the Lord God of Israel, for He hath visited and wrought the redemption of His people.*" ‡ A prisoner rescued from a horrible dungeon through the mercy

---
* John iii. 17. † 1 Peter i. 18, 19. ‡ Luke i. 68.

of his prince feels that he owes a debt of infinite gratitude to his benefactor. And what are our feelings, O devout soul, when we reflect on all that Jesus Christ has done for us? What return ought we not to make for such infinite bounty? Would a holocaust of ten thousand victims suffice to show our gratitude?

O my sweet Saviour, be Thou for ever blessed for having deigned to visit me and to redeem me with Thy most precious Blood! Oh, permit not, I beseech Thee, that through my fault that Blood be shed for me in vain. Behold my soul empurpled with Thy most precious Blood, and guide it to the secure haven of eternal safety. Oh, how bitterly does it grieve me, that I have hitherto corresponded so little with Thy goodness! that, far from loving Thee as Thou hast deserved, I have crucified Thee afresh by my sins. Have pity, O my Lord, on Thy wretched creature, who full of shame and grief for his sins implores again Thy infinite goodness. Ah, woe is me! what would have been my lot at this moment, hadst Thou permitted me to die whilst yet I was Thy enemy? Instead of blessing Thee and partaking of the fruit of Thy passion and death, I should have been compelled to curse and blaspheme that precious Blood which Thou hast shed for my salvation. But, my God, I earnestly beseech Thee, since of Thy infinite mercy Thou hast preserved me from so great an evil, and again offered me Thy grace and Thy love, to, perfect the work which Thou hast begun within me, draw me entirely to Thee and make me wholly Thine own.

O sweetest Mary, remember me before the throne of thy Son; obtain for me the grace to love Him and serve Him for ever.

EJACULATION.— O Blood of my Saviour, inebriate me.

Visit V.

In which we consider Jesus in the Blessed Sacrament as our Mediator.

I. "*The mediator of God and man, the man Christ Jesus.*" * Mortal sin is an act of rebellion of the creature against his Creator, for by it man casts off the yoke of the divine law, and prefers a short momentary satisfaction to the love of his God; he raises between himself and his Lord a wall of separation. "Ye are no longer my people," said the Lord to faithless Israel, "nor am I any more your God, your sins have raised a wall of division between us." Woe to man if after his sin he had been for ever left to himself, for he would have remained perpetually in a state of hatred

---

* 1 Tim. ii. 5.

and enmity with God. But happy, thrice happy are we who possess a Mediator most powerful and most beneficent. Who interposed in your behalf, O devout soul, when you had been so miserable as to offend the divine majesty by your sins? Who vouchsafed to plead your cause before the heavenly Father, to reconcile you with the offended majesty of God? Who but our most loving Jesus? Who but this same Jesus who now calls you with such sweet encouragement into His presence, and is ever ready to nourish you with His own Body in this Sacrament of love? And who is there, I say not of the race of men, but even in the ranks of the highest Seraphim, who could have undertaken such an office, but Jesus Himself? Who but Jesus could have rendered God propitious to us, by presenting Himself before the divine throne. Oh, blessed are those on whose deep misery Jesus has had pity, to whom He has applied the merits of His bitter passion and death upon the cross, and, triumphing over their hardness of heart, made them well pleasing in the sight of His heavenly Father.

II. "*You are come......to Jesus, the Mediator of the New Testament, and to the sprinkling of blood which speaketh better than that of Abel.*"* It was a great glory to the people

---

* Hebr. xii. 22, 24.

of Israel to have had Moses as their mediator with God. But what was their glory when compared with ours, who have as a Mediator the Son of God Himself in His sacred humanity? Moses was only illustrious as being a type of the Mediator of the new covenant, at whose appearance the ancient figures passed away as do the shades of night at the approach of the sun. "You are not come," writes St. Paul in his Epistle to the Hebrews, "to a mountain that might be touched, and a burning fire, and a whirlwind, and darkness, and storms, and the sound of a trumpet, and the voice of words, which they that heard excused themselves that the word might not be spoken to them......But you are come to Mount Sion, and to the city of the living God, the heavenly Jerusalem, and to the company of many thousands of angels ......and to Jesus, the Mediator of the New Testament, and to the sprinkling of blood which speaketh better than that of Abel,"* for the one cried to the Lord for vengeance, the other for mercy.

III. "*No man cometh to the Father but by Me.*"† Jesus Christ is our Mediator, not only because by Him we were reconciled to the Father when we were enemies to Him through our sins, but also because we cannot

---
* Heb. xii. 18, 22, 24.   † John xiv. 6.

make one single step towards eternal life and towards God our Father without His aid. The eternal Father has placed all His complacency in His only-begotten Son, Jesus Christ, and has constituted Him the one means by which souls shall be conducted to His bosom. Wherefore the apostle St. Peter declares that there is no other name under heaven given unto men whereby they may be saved but only the name of Jesus Christ. * Do you not feel then, O devout soul, emotions of the deepest tenderness at this reflection? Will you not offer to God the Father the thanksgiving of your whole heart, that He has vouchsafed you such a Mediator? Will you not break forth in accents of most heartfelt rejoicing, for that grace by which you can at all times freely approach this Divine Mediator in the most Holy Sacrament? Will you not kiss the pavement of the sacred altars, with a soul filled with the most burning love for Him who makes there the place of His rest?

I adore Thee, O sweetest Jesus; prostrate at Thy sacred feet I acknowledge myself worthy of a thousand hells, for having hitherto made so ill a return for all Thy love. What more could I have done to offend Thee, if instead of being my Mediator Thou hadst been my

---

* Acts. iv. 12.

enemy? Ah, woe is me that I have lived so long at a distance from Thee, and attached to the unreal goods of this miserable earth, as if I could find my end, not in loving and glorifying Thee, my only good, but in feeding myself on the filth and ordure of this fleeting perishable world. But Thou, O my dearest Saviour, art rich in mercy. To Thee then do I recommend myself, beseeching Thee to create in me a new heart, and renew a right spirit within me. Oh! thrice happy should I be if I could wholly detach myself from created things, and concentrate all my love in Thee and in Thee alone. This is my earnest desire, this I hope to obtain from Thee, by the merits of Thy most sacred wounds and by that all burning love with which Thy divine heart is filled in the most Holy Sacrament.

O Mary, my sweetest Mother, turn upon me your loving eyes, and obtain for me the grace to be for ever wholly dissolved by this most holy love of Jesus.

EJACULATION.—Pierce me, O Lord, with the dart of Thy love.

Visit VI.

In which we contemplate Jesus Christ in the Blessed Sacrament as our Head.

I. "*He hath made Him Head over all the Church, which is His body.*"* Since Jesus Christ sacrificed His life that He might cleanse to Himself an acceptable people a pursuer of good works, therefore has the eternal Father placed all things under His feet, as St. Paul the apostle declares, and made Him to be Head of His Church. How does Jesus Christ exercise this office of headship over us? Oh, how admirable are the wonders of His bounty towards us, His miserable creatures! With what unspeakable sweetness does He govern us, and communicate to us the inestimable treasures of His grace! As in the human body the head, which is the seat of all the sensitive powers, directs the motions of all the other members, which thence derive their vital force, so, in the mystical body of the Holy Church, the Head, which is Christ, directs and governs all the members, who draw from it that divine influence which vivifies them and enables them to lead a heavenly life. Oh, how ineffable is

---

* Ephes. i. 22, 23.

the bounty of Jesus towards us, how unspeakable is our happiness!

II. "*Who is the head of all Principality and Power.*"* Jesus Christ is not only Head over us who form His Church here below: He is also Head over the angels and archangels, of the Cherubim and Seraphim, and all the blessed legions of paradise. For from the moment He made His first appearance on this earth, when He lay a new-born infant in the manger at Bethlehem, yea, rather from the first instant of His Conception in the virginal womb of Mary, the angels, bowing down in deepest adoration, acknowledged Jesus as their Head. "And when He bringeth in the First-Begotten into the world, He saith: And let all the angels of God adore him." † But now that He has ascended into heaven, and sitteth at the right hand of the Father, He is continually surrounded by legions of angels and blessed souls, who, in profoundest adoration in His sacred presence, cast down their crowns before His throne, and laud and glorify Him eternally, saying: "Worthy is the Lamb that was slain to receive power and divinity and wisdom and strength and honour and glory and benediction." ‡ What shall we say of

---

* Coloss. ii. 10.   † Hebr. i. 6.
‡ Apoc. v. 12.

those multitudes of blessed spirits who continually surround the altars where Jesus deigns to dwell thus familiarly amongst us, and dwells that He may unite Himself to our souls? What wonders would be presented to our sight, were those veils for a moment withdrawn which now hide the glories of our Lord, and were it given us to behold Him revealed to mortal eyes, together with all the heavenly hosts by whom He is surrounded! But, if we may not behold Him with the eyes of the body, let us at least contemplate Him with those of faith, which teach us that here in the sacred Host, He who is the infinite beauty and the infinite good of paradise, is present with us. O my God, what veneration, what unspeakable tenderness ought not this most adorable mystery to excite within us!

III. "*Doing the truth in charity, we may in all things grow up in Him who is the Head, even Christ.*"* Behold then, O devout soul, in what manner we ought to show ourselves worthy members of our great Head, who is Jesus Christ. For this end we ought to walk in the truth, and make ourselves ever more and more like to Him by a most lively and ardent charity. Thus shall we increase ever more in the unction of the Spirit, until we arrive at

---

* Ephes. iv. 15.

that fulness of spiritual life in which we shall be for ever united to our Beloved. But, if we feel that we have not as yet sufficient spiritual strength to rise so high, let us invoke the aid of Him who is our Head, let us beseech Him to pour into us in abundance that water of salvation which wells forth from His sacred wounds, and is a fountain springing up to life eternal.

O my sweetest Jesus, reject me not from Thy Presence, deny me not that draught of the water of life with which Thou dost refresh the beloved members of Thy Body. "Cast me not away from Thy face, and take not Thy Holy Spirit from me."* Hear me, O Lord, as on Mount Tabor Thou didst hear the voice of Thy heavenly Father. Look upon me, O Lord, with those eyes with which from the tree of the cross Thou didst regard Thy most sorrowful Mother. Speak to me with those lips with which in Thy last agony Thou didst console Thy well beloved disciple, St. John. Open Thy heart, O sweetest Lord, and receive mine, that henceforth it may ever burn and consume with Thy holy love. I am indeed most undeserving of such tenderness, but, relying on Thy infinite bounty, I feel certain that Thou wilt not reject the suppli-

---

* Psalm 1. 13.

cations of Thy servant, but wilt give me the grace which I seek.

O Mary, sweetest of Mothers, succour and assist me by Thy all-powerful intercession, that I may dedicate myself without reserve to thy dearest Jesus.

EJACULATION.—Live, Jesus, my love, and Mary, my sweetest hope.

VISIT VII.

In which we consider Jesus in the Blessed Sacrament as our Master.

"*Know you not that......you are not your own? You are bought with a great price.*" * No sooner did our first parents rebel against God, than the devil, that cruel enemy of souls, straightway took possession of their hearts, became their master, and subjected them with all their posterity to the most ruthless bondage. Now who rescued man from this merciless enemy? Who drew him forth from this dismal prison-house? Who burst asunder the iron fetters with which he was bound? Oh, unspeakable goodness of our most sweet Jesus, which has delivered us from our hopeless misery! Appearing in this world clad in our

---

* 1 Cor. vi. 19, 20.

flesh, He engaged in mortal combat with the powers of darkness, vanquished them, and delivered us from their tyranny. "Despoiling the principalities and powers, He hath exposed them confidently in open show, triumphing over them in Himself."* Yes, it was He, our most loving Jesus, who, yielding Himself to the cross and being lifted up from the earth, thus triumphed over the prince of this world and cast him out, drawing all men to Himself. "The prince of this world shall be cast out, and I, if I be lifted up from the earth, will draw all things to Myself."† We are then no longer our own, but we belong to Christ, who has bought us with the price of His own most precious Blood. By this victory which He has gained for us over the slavery of hell, He has acquired a new title of dominion over us, as over the people purchased by His conquest;‡ and we on our part have contracted a new obligation of gratitude and service to our Lord and Master. Whether then we live or die, as the apostle St. Peter says, we are not our own, but belong to Him by the right of conquest. "For none of us liveth to himself; and no man dieth to himself. For whether we live, we live unto the Lord; or whether we die, we

---

* Coloss. ii. 15. † John xii. 31, 32.
‡ 1 Pet. ii. 9.

die unto the Lord. Therefore, whether we live or whether we die, we are the Lord's."*

II. "*He is the Lord of lords.*"† Men of the world commonly think it a great thing to serve some master of exalted rank, especially if they are near his person and can converse easily with him. But what shall we say, who are so highly favoured as to have Jesus Christ for our Master? Who so great as He, at whose name all who dwell in heaven, on earth, and beneath the earth, bend the knee?‡ Who so loving and benignant as He who admits us thus to His presence, and treats familiarly with us as if we were His equals? May we not be said rather to reign than to serve, when we obey so exalted, yet so sweet a Lord? But how many, alas, beguiled by the delusions of passion, cast from them this sweet yoke, and give themselves up anew unto the power of Satan! Oh, blindness! O, unspeakable madness!

III. "*The ox knoweth its owner, and the ass its master's crib, but Israel hath not known Me, and My people hath not understood.*" ‖ O, ungrateful souls! does Jesus exclaim from the sacred tabernacle, O souls impenetrable to love! How long will ye be so hard of heart as thus

---

* Rom. xiv. 7, 8.   † Apoc. xvii. 14.
‡ Philip. ii. 10.   ‖ Isaias i. 3.

to turn your backs upon the Lord to whom you belong, and to run after your vanities and follies? How long will you be more dull and insensible than the very brutes, for they know their master and are grateful to the hand that caresses them? Why will you not come to Me, to Me who burn with desire to enrich you with My graces and to make you eternally blessed? Oh, why will you not engage in good earnest in My service, which alone can render you eternally glorious in heaven?

Oh, my sweet Jesus, how bitterly does it grieve me to have so often offended Thee, instead of loving and serving Thee with all my heart and soul!

Ah, wicked world! traitorous passions! would that my eyes might be turned into two fountains of tears, that I might bitterly weep for my past abominable infidelity. Perish the day, may that night be hid in eternal oblivion, in which I dared first to outrage Thy infinite bounty, O my God. I am resolved from this hour to devote myself wholly to Thy service. Let the world persecute, let hell itself rage against me, I am resolved henceforth to acknowledge no other Master and Lord than Thee, my Sovereign and my only Good. Confirm me, Lord, by Thy efficacious grace, in these my resolutions. Help me to cast far away all love of creatures, and to concentrate my whole heart in Thee alone.

O Mary, my sweetest Mother, receive my soul into your keeping; cause it to be all on fire with holy love.

EJACULATIONS.—I am Thy slave, my dearest, my only Good. Oh, most sweet, most happy chains of my servitude!

VISIT VIII.

In which we contemplate Jesus in the Blessed Sacrament as our King.

I. "*He hath on His garment and on His thigh written, King of kings and Lord of lords.*" There was never, perhaps, on earth, a king more glorious than Solomon. His might and the majesty of his empire have ever been, and will always continue, an object of the highest admiration among men. But what are all the monarchs of this earth compared to the King of heaven, who is present here concealed in this Sacrament of love? To Him who is the King of kings, the supreme Lord of all earthly potentates! To Him by whose might "kings reign and law-givers decree just things," by whom "princes rule and the mighty decree justice."* To Him in whose hands are the hearts of kings, and who turneth them

---

* Prov. viii. 15.

whithersoever He will.* To Him in whose hands are the heavens, the earth, and the abyss beneath. Who is there that can or shall ever be able to draw us from the power of His dominion? For, "if I ascend into heaven Thou art there, O Lord, and if I go down into hell there also do I find Thee, and if on the wings of thought I fly to the uttermost part of the sea, even there also shall Thy hand lead me, and Thy right hand shall hold me." † Oh, how great is the majesty of that King whom we have ever present on our altars! He is the immortal and invisible King of ages, to whom belongeth honour and glory for ever. Before Him all the powers of the earth bow down and obey, and the princes of the heavenly hosts cast their crowns down to the ground. Compare now, O devout soul, the infinite greatness of Jesus with your own meanness and abomination. Alas, is it not an insult for a creature such as I am to present myself before so dread and mighty a sovereign? Oh, how can I bear the presence of so overwhelming a majesty, I who dare not raise my eyes to gaze on the lowest servant of His heavenly court? Oh, why does not my heart burn with shame and grief, when I think of the irreverence which I have so often committed in His presence? Why do not my tears flow in ceaseless

---

* Prov. xxi. 1.   † Ps. cxxxviii. 10.

torrents, when I consider my vile treasons and ingratitude?

II. "*My yoke is sweet and my burden is light.*" It is the right of every sovereign to impose burdens on his subjects. But what is the yoke of our divine King? Oh, who can declare the wonders of His goodness? Well might He have treated us with the severity our sins have deserved; but no, He willed that, where our sins had abounded, there should His grace likewise abound.

The yoke which He has laid upon us is so sweet, that, instead of being a burden, it is rather a consolation to those who willingly take it upon themselves. "Take my yoke upon you," says Jesus, "and learn of me, for I am meek and humble of heart, and you shall find rest for your souls—for my yoke is sweet and my burden is light."* It is true that, to bear this yoke, we must make sacrifices very irksome to our corrupt inclinations; but he that will bend his shoulder to the yoke will find there such assistance and consolation, that the bitterness will be turned to sweetness, and that which is heavy will become light.

III. "*Behold thy King cometh unto thee meek.*" † The kings of this earth are wont to make a great display of the high-sounding titles which indicate their grandeur and their majesty.

---

* Matt. xi. 20, 30. † Matt. xxi. 5.

Now what is the title most dear to our divine King, and in which he takes delight? Oh, who can describe the greatness of His condescension towards such miserable slaves as ourselves! Of all the glorious titles He had a right to claim, He prefers none to that of King of meekness and benignity. Nor is this an empty title, but one justly due to His most stupendous deeds. For how did He act during His mortal life on earth? How does He at present treat with us in this Sacrament of love? What are the laws of His government? What the chains by which He binds His subjects to Him? Are they not the inventions of the most exalted love? "I will draw them," says He by His prophet, "by the cords of Adam with the band of love."* Hosanna, then, let us sing with exulting voice. Hosanna to the Son of David, hosanna to our King. Blessed be He that cometh in the name of the Lord. Hosanna in the highest.

My God and my King, behold me then at Thy feet, beseeching Thee to take entire possession of my heart, and to rule there supreme by Thy holy grace. I kiss with profound veneration those sacred chains which bind me to Thee, to my sovereign Lord, and I have no other desire but to obey Thee perfectly in all things. Oh, happy fortune that

---

* Osee xi. 4.

has made me the subject of the King of heaven, who orders all things for the greater good of His faithful servants! How far better is it to serve Thee, O my God, than to rule the whole world! Oh, never permit me then, most gracious Lord, to cast off Thy sweet yoke, to break Thy bonds, and to withdraw myself from Thy service. My past life has been one of the basest ingratitude, henceforth I long only for the time when I shall be wholly Thine. Reign over me, O Lord, in this life by Thy grace, and in that which is to come by Thy glory.

EJACULATION.—O Lord, rule Thou my heart and soul.

Visit IX.

In which we contemplate Jesus in the Blessed Sacrament as our Legislator.

"*I will give my law in their bowels, and I will write it in their hearts.*"* The people of Israel gloried much in their law-giver, Moses, but far greater is our glory, O devout soul, in having for our law-giver the Son of God Himself, the very Wisdom incarnate, of whom Moses was but a type and shadow. The law of Moses

---

* Jerem. xxxi. 33.

was a law of fear and servitude; the law of Christ is one of love and of grace. The law of Moses was directed chiefly to the senses of men; that of Christ takes possession of their souls. Moses, however sage and holy, could not infuse into the hearts of his people a love of the law which he gave them, and the power to observe its precepts. But our divine legislator has not only given to us the law, but, together with it, has also gifted us with His grace, whereby to love and practise what it teaches. In Christ we have a divine legislator, who has graven His laws upon our inmost soul, and written them in the deepest recesses of our heart.

II. *"Love is the fulfilling of the law."* * See here, O devout soul, what is the spirit, the form, the compendium, and the fulness of the law of Christ. It is no other than holy love, divine charity. All that is commanded, says St. Gregory, the whole law is comprehended in charity. Jesus Christ, after having announced the two great precepts of charity, Himself declares that on these depend all the law and the prophets.† Could He have given a law more sweet and lovely than this? Can we conceive a higher glory and honour than that we should be not only invited but urged

---

* Rom. xiii. 10.   † Matt. xxii. 40.

and even obliged to love a God of such infinite bounty? Whom shall we love if we love not a God who is worthy of an infinite love? To whom shall we consecrate our heart, if not to Him who has created and preserved it, and who alone can satisfy and render it happy? Ah, woe to him who loveth not, since he abideth in death!* If, says St. Paul, any man love not our Lord Jesus Christ, let him be anathema.†

III. "*I will put my Spirit in the midst of you, and make you to walk in my precepts.*"‡ O devout soul, consider well these words, which breathe the sweetness of Paradise. Do they not signify what we see every day fulfilled, and have so often experienced in ourselves? Have we not continually with us present on our altars that good God who, beneath the sacramental species, communicates His grace in such abundance, thus making His law easy of execution? Can we not say with truth, when we have the high privilege worthily to receive that Blessed Sacrament of love, that the charity of God is poured forth in our hearts, by means of the spirit which He hath given us,§ and that, by virtue of this spirit, we find the yoke of Christ easy and His burden light? Oh, happy, thrice happy

---

* 1 John iii. 14. † 1 Cor. xvi. 22.
‡ Ezech. xxxvi. 27. § Rom. v. 5.

are we who live in these blessed days, in which together with the law is given also the grace by which to observe it! But, alas, how few are there who prize their high privilege; how many who, instead of using these graces for their sanctification, make them an occasion of offence to their Lord, by reason of their ingratitude!

I bless Thee, O Lord Almighty, Father of Jesus Christ my Saviour, and I return Thee my most hearty thanks for that Thou hast vouchsafed to give me Thine only-begotten Son, to be to me a law-giver most holy and most mighty. O Lord, look upon the face of Thy Christ,* and, by reason of His abundant merits, grant me grace faithfully to keep Thy holy law. Pour forth, O God, Thy Holy Spirit upon me, and make me to walk in the way of Thy commandments. Draw me to Jesus, my Lord, with the sweet chains of Thy love, and suffer me not at any time to fall away from Him. O Jesus, my most sweet Lord, take me within Thine arms, hold me in Thy bosom, hide me within the hollow of Thy side, that I may wholly turn away from the things of this world and give all my thoughts to Thee. Punish me for my sins, afflict me as Thou wilt for my ingratitude— but Thy holy love, O Lord, take not away

* Ps. lxxxiii. 10.

from me. Give to me, O Lord, Thy love together with Thy grace, and behold I am rich enough, and ask of Thee nothing more. *

EJACULATION.—O Lord, write Thou Thy law in the midst of my heart.

VISIT X.

In which we contemplate Jesus in the Blessed Sacrament as our True Lover.

I. "*I have loved thee with an everlasting love.*"† Who was it, O devout soul, that first loved you ? Was it your father or your mother? Ah, no ; it was Jesus Christ Himself. Before your parents themselves were born, Jesus loved you. Before the earth existed, or any of the creatures that are in it, Jesus loved you. He loved you before time, from all eternity. "I have loved thee with a perpetual love." The prophet David marvelled that the Lord should deign to have regard to man. But what should be our astonishment when we consider that our most sweet Jesus not only is mindful of us, but that He has borne us written on His heart from all eternity, and has thought of us for our good before all time began ? He who is unmoved at this thought either is without

---

* S. Ignatius. † Jerem. xxxi. 3.

faith or has a heart of stone. Oh, then let us love our dearest Lord, since He loved us first of all. "Let us love God, because He first loved us."*

II. "*He who loved me, and delivered Himself for me.*" † The love which Christ bears to us is no sterile love of mere words, but is a love strong and mighty in deeds. What but His love for us led Him to clothe Himself with our mortality and to become Man? What moved Him to take upon Himself all our miseries and to suffer for us? What was it that nailed Him to a cross and made Him die upon it? Ah, devout soul, full well do we know the cause. It was His too great love for us—it was nothing else but His excessive love. As it was this love for us which moved the Eternal Father to send into the world His well-beloved Son for our redemption, so it was the same love which moved that Divine Son Himself to become Man, to suffer, to hang in agony, and at last to die for us upon the cross.

Oh, how then can we be so insensible to this excess of love? How is it that our hearts do not glow with the fire of charity at the thought of a God scourged and dying for love of us? Alas, we think but seldom of this stupendous mystery of love, and hence it is

---

* 1 John iv. 19.   † Gal. ii. 20.

that we are languid and cold in our love of our most loving Jesus. Let us then cast away our tepidity, and give all our love to Him who has done so much to gain it. Let us not forget those great words of St. Paul, that Jesus died for all, that they who live may not now live to themselves, but "unto Him who died for them."*

III. "*Jesus, knowing that His hour was come, that He should pass out of this world to the Father; having loved His own, who were in the world, He loved them unto the end.*" † Behold with awe and astonishment, O devout soul, the piteous sight of thy sweet Jesus, His sacred body one wound from head to foot. Behold Him overwhelmed with insults and barbarously nailed to the cross. What more could He have done to prove His love to you? Are not these the utmost limits which even His immense charity could reach? Rise, then, O loving souls, and filled with sacred ardour tell ye to all people the admirable inventions of your loving and beloved Jesus. The mystery of the cross, great and stupendous though it be, was yet insufficient to satisfy the ineffable tenderness of that loving heart. The charity of that divine heart urged Him yet further to greater excesses of love. Raise then your eyes, O devout soul; fix them upon yonder

---

* 2 Cor. v. 15.   † John xiii. 1.

altar, and within that sacred tabernacle you will discover the greatest triumph of Jesus' love towards us. That most sacred Host, deprived as it is in appearance of all splendour and dignity, is the very masterpiece of divine bounty, and the compendium of all the greatest marvels of God's love to man. "He hath made a remembrance of His wonderful works, being a merciful and gracious Lord. He hath given Food to them that fear Him."* By means of that most Sacred Host, the Son of God made man dwells continually with us, communicates Himself to our souls, and perpetuates in the midst of us the same ineffable mystery which He once consummated on the cross. This is, in fine, the greatest prodigy of the divine goodness, and the greatest pledge of His love that a God of infinite charity could have given to man. And does not one who is insensible to such an excess of love deserve to be an object of universal abhorrence?

O my God, what confusion, what shame to me, when I consider how often and how long I have been ungrateful to Thy infinite bounty! How was it possible that I could have had the cruelty to rebel against the goodness of my Lord, and to afflict so bitterly

---

* Psalm cx. 4, 5.

His most loving heart? Oh, horrible blindness! See here your most loving Saviour, who stretches out His arms towards you, and calls you to His bosom; and you, instead of answering His call, have turned your back upon Him, and despised all His graces. He has prepared for you a saving bath of His own most sacred blood to wash your guilt away; and you, instead of availing yourself of it to cleanse your soul, have trampled it beneath your feet.

He has provided for you the food of paradise, His own sacred body; and you have turned from it to wallow in the mire of all uncleanness. In fine, while He has thought and provided for your life in a thousand ways, you, instead of showing yourself grateful for His goodness, have risen up against Him, and crucified Him again by your sins. Oh, who will give a fountain of tears to my eyes?* Who will grant that my contrition and bitterness of heart shall exceed the sea itself in magnitude? Pardon, O my God, pardon this miserable creature. Heal me with Thy saving grace, and grant me henceforth to love Thee as much as I have hitherto offended Thee. I desire nothing from this day forward but to live and die in peace

---

* Jer. ix. 1.

with Thee, and to unite myself for ever to Thy holy love.

EJACULATION.—O Lord, grant that I may faithfully respond to Thy holy love.

Visit XI.

In which we contemplate Jesus in the Blessed Sacrament as our Benefactor.

I. "*He went about doing good.*" * Consider the feelings of mercy, of tenderness, of pity, and of liberality with which Jesus Christ, during His mortal life, went about doing good —giving sight to the blind, healing the sick, raising the dead to life, and pouring out blessings on all who approached Him. These He now feels, and even more strongly, in this Sacrament of love. Picture to yourself a great fire enclosed within a narrow furnace; with what ardour and intensity does it not burn! Such may you imagine the heart of Jesus to be in the most Blessed Sacrament. Think how it suffers, if we may say so, an inexpressible agony of pain through the excessive fulness of grace with which it is filled, and to which it cannot give vent, not finding hearts disposed to receive it. Our Lord one

* Acts x. 38.

day spake thus to a devout soul, showing her, from that throne of love, His heart like an abyss of fire: "Assist me," said Jesus, "dear daughter, relieve me of some part of this burden. Publish to the world, and cause to be proclaimed throughout the whole earth, that I set no bounds to the graces which I bestow on those souls who come to seek for them from this loving heart of mine." O ye sons of men! how long will ye be hard of heart? How long will ye run after vanity and deceit? Unhappy beings, what do you hope for from those goods which you so eagerly seek, and for which you spend your labour and your strength, but bitterness and affliction of spirit? Open, then, your eyes before it be too late; lament your dire delusion; raise your heart to objects worthy of its love; and place all your hopes of peace and satisfaction in Jesus alone.

II. "*If any man thirst, let him come to Me and drink.*" Oh, how many are the sweet invitations which Jesus Christ makes to us from His throne of love, calling us to Him that He may enrich us with His graces. He that thirsteth, let him come unto Me and drink. Whosoever shall drink of the water that I will give, shall not thirst for ever. Because the water that I shall give him shall be within his heart a fountain of living water springing up to life eternal.* Come to me, all ye whose lips are parched with thirst, and I will give you to drink. I will refresh you.† "All ye that thirst come to the waters."‡ Draw near to Me, and draw from My pierced side the waters of eternal life. Ye shall draw waters with joy from the Saviour's fountain.§ Like a mother whose breasts are filled with milk, and who goes abroad seeking for children whom she may take to her bosom, so in like manner does Jesus in the Blessed Sacrament invite all to come to Him and to draw from His sacred breast the milk of paradise. Oh, what return shall we then make to our good Lord for the favours of His infinite bounty? When holy Tobias beheld his son return home from his long journey, he was overpowered by the consideration of the innumerable favours and benefits which his son had received from the angel who accompanied him, and whom he took merely for a holy man. He called his son to him and said, "What can we give to this holy man, that is come with thee?" Tobias answering, said to his father, "Father, what wages shall we give him? or what can be worthy of his benefits?... What can we give him sufficient for these things?" But when they understood that their benefactor

---

* John iv. 14. † John vii. 37.
‡ Isai. lv. 1. § Isai. xii. 3.

D

was an angel from heaven, then, indeed, says the Scripture, lying prostrate for three hours upon their face, they blessed God: and rising up, they told all His wonderful works.* If, then, the consideration of the favours which they had received from a creature made so great an impression on the hearts of these holy men, what emotions ought we not to feel within us at the thought that we have been so unspeakably favoured by our Creator and Redeemer Himself? If they blessed the Lord for this visit of His angel, what ought we to do, who have with us continually, not indeed an angel, but the King of angels and of saints, the very Son of God made man? Oh, let us bless the God of heaven, and give glory to Him in the presence of all that live, because, in giving to us His Divine Son in the most Holy Sacrament, He hath shown forth His great mercy towards us. †

III. "*What is there that I ought to do more to my vineyard, that I have not done to it?*" ‡ What more could our most loving Jesus have done for us, that He has not done? Has He not magnified His mercy towards us, and poured forth upon us His graces in abundance? What return have we made to this infinite goodness? Ah, thankless

---

* Tob. xii. 22.
† Tob. xii. 6.   ‡ Isai. v. 4.

hearts, does He exclaim from these sacred altars, hearts which know not love. I have rescued you from the slavery of hell; and you, instead of showing yourself faithful servants of your lawful Master, have done nothing but afflict Me with outrages. I have planted you in the fair garden of my Church, and you, instead of bearing fruit to life eternal, have produced nothing but thorns and brambles. I have fed you with the manna of My sacred body, and you have given me in return gall and vinegar. I have prepared for you a royal diadem, and you have pierced My head with a bitter crown of thorns. I have raised you up from your low estate, and you have crucified Me on a shameful gibbet." *

Oh, mercy, Jesus, full of pity; mercy for this miserable creature! Alas, I grieve from my very heart for having made so ill a return for Thy unspeakable goodness. But oh! cease not to pour out Thy benefits upon me. If I have hitherto so much abused Thy favours, I am now resolved that it shall be so no longer; I will use them for Thy glory and my own sanctification. Enlighten my eyes with one ray of Thy heavenly light, whereby I may discern more clearly the vanity of all things of this earth, and the inestimable price of the things of heaven. Pour forth of Thy

* Holy Church in the Office of Good Friday.

Holy Spirit into my heart, and make it to become a perfect victim of Thy love. I desire most earnestly to be detached from every created thing, to die to the world and to its vanities, and to live to Thee and to Thee alone. Oh, happy, thrice happy should I be, could I love Jesus, my sweetest Lord, with my whole heart and soul and mind.

O Mary, Mother most sweet and tender, to you I commit myself. I pray you obtain for me this grace from your beloved Son Jesus.

EJACULATION.—Pour forth, O Lord, Thy grace into my heart.

Visit XII.

In which we contemplate Jesus in the Blessed Sacrament as our Father.

I. "*Thy children like olive plants round about Thy table.*"* Amongst the various titles with which our Divine Saviour condescends to address those who come to Him in full confidence in His divine goodness and power, one is that of children. "Children," He said to the apostles, "how hard is it for those who trust in riches to enter into the kingdom of God." †

---

* Psalm cxxvii. 3.   † Mark x. 24.

"Be of good heart, son," He said to the man sick of the palsy, "thy sins are forgiven thee."* This title of sons, by which Jesus Christ addressed his followers, belongs not to them so much as the offspring of His hands, because He has given to them their natural life, as because He has regenerated them in the waters of baptism, and there breathed into their souls the supernatural life of grace. Hence, since it is certain that by means of holy baptism we were born to the new life by virtue of the grace of Christ, in which we were truly regenerated or born again, we are therefore become truly His children, and He has become verily and indeed our Father. Wherefore Isaias, speaking in the spirit of prophecy, says of Him, "For a Child is born to us, and a Son is given to us, and the government is upon His shoulders. And His name shall be called Wonderful, Counsellor, God the Mighty, *the Father of the World to come*, the Prince of Peace." †

It is in the Blessed Sacrament of the Eucharist that this loving Father most clearly displays His paternal care and treats most tenderly with His children. For in this Divine Sacrament it is that He presses them to His bosom, instructs, consoles, sustains

---
* Matt. ix. 2.   † Isai. ix. 6.

them with the Bread of Life. Rejoice, O devout soul, in the possession of so good, so tender, so loving a Father. Where shall we find an earthly father whose tenderness towards his children approaches to His? What is a mother's tenderest love compared to that which Jesus bears to His children? For it is thus He speaks by His prophet Isaias, saying that a mother may indeed forget the fruit of her womb, but He will never forget us. "If she should forget, yet will I not forget thee." * "Behold I have graven thee in My hands, † and upon My heart. Thou art to Me as the pupil of Mine eye. He that toucheth thee toucheth the apple of Mine eye." ‡

II. "*My son, give me thy heart.*" § Behold, O devout soul, what it is that Jesus asks of you. He asks not that you afflict your body with rough hair-cloths, that bread and water should be your best repast, that you hide yourself from the face of men in some solitary cavern, or go to dwell with the beasts of the wilderness. No, all He asks of you is to give Him your heart. He does not expect you for His love to pass your life in perpetual weeping, or give yourself up a prey to continual unceasing insults and

---

* Isai. xlix. 15. † Isai. xlix. 16.
‡ Zach. ii. 8. § Prov. xxiii. 26.

injuries; He only wills that you take Him for the sole object of all your affection and of all your labours. He wishes, in fine, that you love Him with the true affection of a son; that so He may press you to His bosom with the true affection of a Father. Could He have made a request more tender, more sweet, more loving than this? Ah, would that we understood aright what it is to give our heart to a God of infinite goodness; then should we feel so moved to tenderness that we should even be ravished out of ourselves at the very thought! Who can express the infinite good possessed by him who reposes in the bosom of his God, who forms the delight of the heart of his God? Why, then, O devout soul, do you not correspond better to the sweet invitation of Jesus to give Him your heart? Does He not indeed deserve that we consecrate ourselves wholly to His glory and His honour? Has He not a thousand titles to our warmest gratitude, to our most ardent love?—He who is infinite beauty, sweetness, goodness, so that, had we a thousand hearts to consecrate to Him, it would be all too little, and we should yet be all too far from loving Him as much as He deserves. How then can we dare refuse this one heart which we have to give, and which we know that He holds so dear?

III. "*The son honoureth the father . . . . if then I be a Father, where is My honour? . . . . saith the Lord of Hosts.*"* Since we have in Jesus Christ a Father so infinitely great and good, it is our strict obligation to honour Him with our whole heart. But how have we fulfilled this obligation? If He is our Father, where is the honour we have paid him? Oh, monstrous ingratitude of men! "I have brought up children and exalted them," He exclaims from yonder sacred Tabernacle, "and they have despised me." † With shame and confusion, let us bow down and humble ourselves to the dust before our Father; let us return Him hearty thanks that He has not in chastisement of our ingratitude for ever cancelled our names from the number of His children. Indeed, we have because of our unfaithfulness deserved to be driven from His sight for ever, and condemned to pay the penalty of our baseness in eternal torments. But see, our good Father has not only borne with us patiently, He has even continued to pour forth His graces upon us and to treat us as His beloved children.

O most beloved Jesus, behold at Thy feet an ungrateful prodigal, who, covered with shame and confusion, returns to his Father, grieved for having offended so good and tender

---

* Mal. i. 6. † Isai. i. 2.

a Father. Verily, I deserve not to be called Thy son. But, O good Jesus, supply for my unworthiness from the fountain of Thy infinite mercy. Permit me once more to throw myself into Thy arms. Oh, press me once again to Thy bosom, and give me leave to call Thee, as of old, by the sweet name of Father. Deprive me, if Thou wilt, of the sweet and sensible consolation of Thy presence, reserved for those innocent souls who have always been faithful to Thee. Take not away from me Thy love and Thy grace. Remember that, although I deserve not any longer to be numbered amongst Thy children, because of my offences, yet Thou hast not ceased to be my Father. Despise not, O Lord, the work of Thy own hands. Grant that, as out of Thy infinite bounty I have been made partaker of the life of grace in this world, so I may receive in like manner the life of glory in the world to come.

O Mary, my Mother and my sweetest hope, pray for me, and never more permit me to offend your Divine Son.

EJACULATION.—O my Jesus, have pity on Thy ungrateful child.

Visit XIII.

In which we contemplate Jesus in the Blessed Sacrament as our Brother.

I. "*The first-born among many brethren.*" * Jesus Christ is not only our Father, but He is also most truly our Brother. He is our Father inasmuch as He has begotten us anew to the life of grace; He is also our Brother, inasmuch as, regenerating us to the life of grace, He has made us the adopted sons of God and also His brethren by adoption. "You have not," saith St. Paul, "received the spirit of bondage again in fear, but you have received the spirit of adoption of sons, whereby we cry: Abba (Father)." †
"Behold," saith St. John, "what manner of charity the Father hath bestowed upon us, that we should be called and should be the sons of God." ‡ And again in the beginning of his Gospel he says, "As many as received Him, He gave them power to be made the sons of God." § What sweet hope and joy should we not conceive when we consider that we have in Jesus Christ a Brother so tender and so loving.

---

* Rom. viii. 29.　　† Rom. viii. 15.
‡ 1 John iii. 1.　　§ John i. 12.

II. "*And about him was the ring of his brethren.*"* Great was the goodness of Joseph, who, when exalted to be Viceroy of Egypt, instead of taking revenge on his brethren as he might easily have done, not only pardoned them the grievous injuries which they had formerly inflicted on him, but with brotherly tenderness called them to his arms, pressed them to his bosom, and received them with especial favour. But the bounty and goodness of Joseph towards his brethren is only a figure of that which Jesus Christ continually exhibits towards us. Who can number the injuries which ungrateful Christians inflict every moment on that sweetest and tenderest of hearts? How many are there who commit the most horrible outrages against His adorable person, and as far as it is in their power crucify him afresh by their sins! How many acts of ingratitude and infidelity does He not every day receive at the hand of those whom He has more especially benefitted, and who should serve Him with greater perfection! How many souls are there to whom He has shown an especial predilection, drawing them from out the dangers of the world and placing them in the road to sanctity, but who, instead of corresponding to His goodness, are insensible to His favours and even dare to

---

* Ecclus. l. 13.

offend him grievously! But in what manner does He treat these ungrateful souls? Does He treat them with indignation? Does He launch against them the arrows of His wrath? Does He reject or at least refuse to admit them to His sacred presence? Ah, no; on the contrary He ceases not to treat them with His wonted tenderness, and to visit them with His graces; to invite them sweetly to His arms, and to make ready for them the Food of Paradise. Is it not thus, indeed, that Jesus has treated you, O devout soul, when turning from your sins you have cast yourself at His feet and implored His pardon? Did He meet you with reproaches? Was He not on the contrary all tenderness and pity? O my soul, bless thou for ever the name of the Most High, in that He has given thee a Brother so infinitely loving and bounteous! Consider how in the Blessed Sacrament Jesus Christ shows forth most clearly His loving bounty and brotherly tenderness. For it is in this Divine Sacrament that He treats most familiarly with us, He makes us sit with Him at table, He imparts His favours and graces to us; He inflames us with His love and unites Himself most intimately with our souls. Ah, thrice blessed are we, who can at any moment treat with this most loving Brother, lay open to Him our whole hearts, beseech Him to inspire us with His graces, and to unite us even more closely to Himself.

III. "*Whosoever shall do the will of my Father that is in heaven, he is my brother.*"* The foundation of our union with Jesus Christ as our Brother consists wholly in the likeness which we bear to Him, and in the intimate union of our souls with Him by means of divine grace. For this it is which makes us the children of God, and renders us beloved in the eyes of our heavenly Father, who loves us with a supernatural love only in so far as we are one with His Beloved Son, our Lord Jesus Christ. Whoever, then, wishes to be bound in the sweet chain of brotherhood with Jesus Christ must above all things be faithful to grace, and conform his will to that of his Lord. Be not deceived, dearly beloved, exclaims Jesus, from the sacred Tabernacle. Mere words and empty protestations of love will not suffice to make you partakers of the grace of brotherhood with Me: deeds and acts of generosity are required. It is necessary that all vicious inclinations should be repressed, all disorderly affections should be renounced and your whole heart sacrificed to Me by conforming in all things to My will. "He that doth the will of My Father, who is in heaven, he

---

* Matt. xii. 50.

is My brother;" without this, the title of brother will be a mere empty name, which will only increase your confusion at the day of judgment.

Oh yes, my dearest Lord, I do earnestly desire to wage continual war with my passions, and to consecrate my whole being to Thy holy love. O God of my heart, I grieve for having offended Thee; I have long enough been ungrateful to Thy infinite bounty; but now I am resolved to seek no other consolation, no other good but Thee, my Life, my Treasure, my All. Oh, pour forth Thy Holy Spirit upon me, that I may become worthy of brotherhood with Thee, and an object of complacency in the eyes of my heavenly Father. Cleanse my soul with Thy precious Blood, inflame it with Thy divine charity. O Jesus, regard not my infidelities, think only of Thy love and tender compassion. Free me from sin by virtue of Thy sacred wounds, and give me grace to become a saint.

O Mary, my sweetest Mother, come to my succour; obtain for me this grace from your Divine Son, that I may live and die in His holy love.

EJACULATION.—O Lord, Thy will be done on earth as it is in heaven.

Visit XIV.

In which we contemplate Jesus in the Blessed Sacrament as our Friend.

I. "*Eat, O my friends, and drink and be inebriated, my dearly beloved.*"* Who could ever have imagined that the God of majesty and glory, the King of heaven and earth, should so condescend to His miserable creatures as to dwell continually in the midst of them, and invite them to share His friendship? Yet what it would have seemed folly even to imagine, we see actually before our eyes in this Blessed Sacrament of love. What could we desire to find in the tenderest and best of friends, which we possess not in a most eminent and perfect degree in our sweet Lord Jesus? In the first place, He loves us with a most ardent love, insomuch that, although His greatness and magnificence are without bounds, yet does He delight in dwelling amongst us. "My delights," says He, "were to be with the sons of men."† He is, moreover, ever ready to dispense His graces to us in abundance; and from these sacred altars He continually invites us to come to Him, that He may enrich us with His favours.

---

* Cant. v. 1.   † Prov. viii. 31.

Moreover, He illuminates our minds with His heavenly light, and reveals to us His hidden secrets. For He declared to His apostles, and repeats now from the sacred Tabernacle to the loving soul: "I will not now call you servants, for the servant knoweth not what his lord doth; but I have called you friends, because all things whatsoever I have heard of my Father, I have made known to you."[*] In fine, He invites us continually to His sacred bosom, and burns with the desire of taking a lasting possession of our souls. Come unto Me My well-beloved friends, does He exclaim in this Sacrament of love; come unto Me, eat, drink and be inebriated. The food wherewith My sacred board is spread is My own body, and the drink is My own most sacred blood. Eat, then, and drink, that so we may become but one in the bond of love. "He that eateth My flesh and drinketh My blood, abideth in Me and I in him."[†] Oh, infinite condescension! Oh, love unspeakable! Oh, abyss of charity!

II. "*A faithful friend is a strong defence; and he that hath found him hath found a treasure.*"[‡] Amongst men it is accounted a great thing to have any connexion, however distant, with the great ones of the earth, and

---

[*] John xv. 15.
[†] John vi. 57.   [‡] Ecclus. vi. 14.

especially with kings and princes. And they who receive from them any particular mark of friendship are quite elated with joy, and imagine themselves to have arrived at the very summit of glory. The proud Haman " called together to him his friends and Zara his wife, and he declared unto them, saying, ...Queen Esther also hath invited no other to the banquet with the king but me, and with her I am also to dine to-morrow with the king." * No sacrifice is so great, or labour so troublesome, that a man will not undergo it in order to procure a distinguished place at court, so that he may recommend himself in some degree to the notice of his sovereign. If, then, the friendship of earthly princes is so much valued, how greatly ought we not to esteem the friendship of the King of heaven? If to gain the friendship of the noble and the great, no sacrifice is considered too much, what sacrifices should we not be ready to make to acquire the friendship of the Sovereign of the universe? Compared with Jesus Christ, what are all the monarchs of this earth but dust and ashes? Shall we then be cold and languid in our efforts to become the friends of so great a King, in comparison with whom all the sovereigns of the earth are as though they had never been? Shake off

---

* Esther v. 10.

then, O devout soul, your sluggishness of spirit, and resolve to concentrate your whole being in Jesus; to take him for the dearest friend of your heart. Blessed will you be if you shall have placed all your love in Him, for in Him you will find a sure comfort and stay in the time of need. "Blessed is he that findeth a true friend." * Leaning on such a friend, you shall securely pass through this life, and shall not fear to enter into the very shadow of death. Bind yourself close to Jesus, and you shall find in Him at all times a faithful friend, a powerful protector, and a heavenly treasure.

III. "*You are my friends if you do the things which I command you.*" † In order to gain the friendship of earthly monarchs, it is not enough merely to desire it; sometimes even the greatest sacrifices do not suffice. How many, after having gone through great difficulties, impaired their health and spent the best part of their life in the pursuit of distinction, have found themselves at the end immersed in a sea of cares, and as far as ever from the object of their desires? Far different is it with those who aspire to the friendship of the King of kings; a sincere desire will secure it. The friendship of the great is not granted to all, and the few who

---

* Ecclus. xxv. 12.   † John xv. 14.

gain it esteem themselves singularly privileged; but it is not so with the friendship of Jesus, for this all men can obtain, whatever be their condition, be they rich or poor, noble or plebeian. The friendship of earthly sovereigns cannot be gained in an instant; but the friendship of Jesus Christ can be acquired in one moment. "Behold," said that courtier of whom St. Augustine speaks in his Confessions, "at this very moment I may become, if I will, the friend of God." For, to become the friend of Jesus Christ, all that is required is a firm resolution and will to keep His holy law. You shall be my friends, said this most loving Saviour to His apostles, if you keep My commandments. This is the one necessary condition for attaining to the friendship of our Lord Jesus Christ. "If you love Me," He says from the sacred Tabernacle, "keep My commandments."* "He that hath My commandments and keepeth them, he it is that loveth Me."† Enter now into yourself, O devout soul, and examine well what care you take to observe His laws with fidelity. What are your affections, your aim, your intentions? Can you say that in all your actions you follow no other rule than the holy will of God; that you love nothing except in reference to God? Search then your heart

---
* John xiv. 15. † John xiv. 21.

with all diligence, and whatever faults you discover, however light they may be, apply yourself earnestly to destroy them; for, although light infractions of the law of God do not deprive us of the divine friendship, they tend nevertheless to weaken its strength and chill its ardour, and but too often expose the soul to the danger of losing it altogether.

I thank Thee, O most sweet Jesus, for Thy infinite goodness in treating me as Thy friend. But what am I? And what art Thou, my God? Am I not a miserable creature, unworthy of Thy grace, deserving of nothing but chastisement? Art not Thou a God of infinite majesty, deserving of infinite homage and love? How then can it be that Thou shouldst so abase Thyself as to unite me to Thee, and raise me to the dignity of a friend? Oh, blessed for ever be Thy infinite goodness, O God of my heart! For ever blessed be that most loving heart, which so burns with love for such a miserable worm. Blessed be Thy most holy wounds, Thy blood, Thy death, which are to me as a mine of inexhaustible treasure. I love Thee, O God of my heart. I desire to live and to die only for Thy love.

O Mary, my most sweet Mother, cast upon me a pitying glance. Oh, obtain for me the grace to love your divine Son for ever and ever.

EJACULATION.—O sweet Jesus, melt my hard heart, kindle it with Thy holy love.

VISIT XV.

In which we contemplate Jesus in the Blessed Sacrament as our Spouse.

I. "*I will espouse Thee to me in faith.*"* Why did Jesus assume our human nature, and clothe Himself with our infirmities? Why did He pour out His most precious blood, and undergo the painful death of the cross? What was the design of His most loving heart in suffering such afflictions, and in all the miracles and wonderful works which He continues to show forth in the Sacrament of His love? Who could believe it possible, did not faith assure us of it! Jesus Christ did and suffered so much, in order to celebrate His heavenly espousal with our souls, and to contract with them the most intimate union. This is a wonderful and stupendous mystery, but yet most true. The soul of the just is indeed the beloved spouse of Jesus Christ, and He is her Beloved. This espousal is wholly spiritual and heavenly, founded upon faith, formed by charity; it has its beginning in this

---

* Osee ii. 20.

life through grace, and its consummation in the next life in glory.

II. "*Can the children of the bridegroom mourn as long as the bridegroom is with them.*"* How consoling are these words to those loving souls who have taken Christ for their Spouse! What greater blessing could they desire in this life, than to have evermore present with them in this Sacrament of love the dear object of their holy affection, their most loving Jesus? What joy ought they not to feel at having this beloved Spouse so near at hand, that they can visit Him whenever they please, open to Him their hearts, and pour forth the loving affection of their souls! What consolation, what happiness! Here reflect, O devout soul, that Jesus Christ is not the Spouse of innocent souls only, but even of penitents. As He condescended to give the name of bride to St. Catherine of Siena, that most pure virginal soul who had always kept unsullied the white robe of her baptismal innocence, so also did He deign to confer the same title on St. Margaret of Cortona, once a great sinner, but afterwards an illustrious penitent. It is true, indeed, that sin impresses on the soul a mark of infamy, which renders it an object of abhorrence in the eyes of Jesus; but by His grace these

* Matt. ix. 15.

filthy stains are washed away, and the soul becomes again an object of complacency to its Lord.

III. "*Behold the Bridegroom cometh, go ye out to meet Him.*"* What a consolation to loving souls is the consideration that their sweet Spouse, Who at present conceals Himself beneath the sacramental veils, will come to meet them at the end of their mortal life, clothed in all the splendour of His glory, to call them to His embrace, and to celebrate with them an eternal union of love! What joy will then be theirs, when they behold unveiled their most adorable and loving Lord, in Whose bosom they will find their eternal repose? But remember, O devout soul, that our loins must be girt, and our lamps must be burning in our hands, † if we desire to go forth with gladness to meet the Bridegroom, and to be received by Him with the love of a Spouse. We must have our consciences pure and undefiled, and our heart must burn with the heavenly fire of charity. Thus prepared, we shall joyfully meet Jesus when He approaches, and He will receive us in triumph; but woe to us, if we venture to meet Him unprepared; for He will close the door upon us, and drive us from His face, like the foolish virgins of the Gospel.

* Matt. xxv. 6.   † Luke xii. 35.

Oh, permit me not, dear Jesus, I beseech Thee, to present myself before Thee without having first cleansed away the filth from this heart, and done worthy fruits of penance. Since Thou hast done and suffered so much in order to unite to Thyself this soul of mine, oh! give me grace to die to every created thing, and to live to Thee alone. O divine fire, inflame my heart, and consume in Thy ardent flame whatever Thou seest disorderly or vicious within me. Grant that my soul may love Thee, and remain ever united to Thee in this life, that so, in the life to come, it may consummate together with Thee those eternal nuptials of love which will form its never-ending felicity and blessedness. Would that I could love Thee, my dearest Lord, as much as Thou deservest to be loved. But since this, alas! is impossible, let me at least love Thee as much as I am able. Yes, my most loving Jesus, be Thou my love, my only, my sweetest love. I am resolved to live and to die only for Thy love.

O Mary, my Mother, best of all beloved, help me, I beseech thee, and kindle within this heart true love of thy dear Son Jesus.

EJACULATION.—Take into Thine own hands, O sweetest Jesus, this soul of mine; govern it and direct it evermore according to the good pleasure of Thy will.

Visit XVI.

In which we contemplate Jesus in the Blessed Sacrament as our Master.

I. *"One is your Master, Christ."* * In what condition was the world respecting the knowledge of the truth before Christ's coming? With the exception of the Jewish nation the whole world was involved in one universal mist of ignorance and error. We are astounded at the absurdities propounded even by those amongst the ancients most esteemed for their wisdom; and what shall we say of the wild delusion indulged in by the ignorant on the most essential points of religion? But blessed a thousand times be the charity of Christ our Saviour, Who, having made Himself man, has become our Master, and called us out of darkness into His marvellous light! † He who is Himself the True Light which enlighteneth every man that cometh into the world, ‡ has diffused around the rays of His heavenly wisdom, and renewed in a short time the whole face of the earth. Taught by such a Master, the unlearned, the ignorant are far better instructed in what belongs to the soul,

---

* Matt. xxiii. 10.
† 1 Pet. ii. 9.   ‡ John i. 9.

and in what concerns God and eternity, than the most renowned philosopher of antiquity.

Everything in those days was made matter of dispute; and yet, after most vehement discussion of the fundamental maxims of religion, even those most distinguished among them for wisdom found themselves involved in never-ending contradictions and obscurity. But since Jesus Christ has appeared amongst us, and instructed us in His heavenly doctrine, truth has become bright, clear, and manifest, not merely to the learned, but even to the most unlettered, provided only they bring with them to the study a humble and docile heart. What ought not to be our gratitude for so infinite a benefit.

II. "*This is my beloved Son, in whom I am well pleased: hear ye Him.*" * We have for our Teacher, not an angel or an archangel, but the very Son of God Himself, consubstantial with the Father, and made Man for the love of us. The apostle St. Paul, speaking of this display of God's love to us, says, "God, Who at sundry times, and in diverse manners, spoke in times past to our fathers by the prophets, last of all, in these days, hath spoken to us by His Son." † This divine Teacher with His own mouth instructed us during the course of His mortal life, and

---

* Matt. xvii. 5. † Hebr. i. 1.

now that He has withdrawn Himself from our bodily eyes, He still continues to teach us in many and marvellous ways, and chiefly by means of His Church, which He has established to the end of time as the pillar and foundation of truth. Great, then, is our happiness in having such a Master. Can we find, or even imagine to ourselves, a better Master? For is He not the Light of the world? Has He not the word of eternal life? Is not His teaching infallible and divine? Why, then, do we not listen with docility to His instructions? Why do we not humbly submit to His teaching? Why do we not profoundly revere His precepts? Ah, woe to the proud, woe to those unhappy souls who refuse to hearken to the sweet Teacher of wisdom.

III. "*He has given to Him the science of the saints.*" * What does our divine Master teach us? In what science, O devout soul, does He instruct His beloved? Those holy souls well know it who enjoy the happiness of learning in the school of Christ, and of drinking in His heavenly doctrine. The science which He teaches is from heaven, and is directed to lead men thither, and to render them eternally blessed. It is not a science which puffeth up, but which edifieth : † a science which inspires nothing but justice and sanctity. The

---

* Wisd. x. 10.   † 1 Cor. viii. 1.

principal points of this science are, a contempt of the world and of its vanities, a detachment of the heart from all created objects, the value of suffering for justice' sake, and the strict union of the soul with God. Its disciples are the true children of the light, and they who oppose it are blind in very deed, and are such as sit in darkness and in the shadow of death. * This is that science whereby the desert has been peopled with solitaries, the cloisters with religious, and the world with just men, who, while they lived in the world according to the body, had their heart and their conversation in heaven. † Enlightened from above by this heavenly science, virgins have kept their pure souls spotless before God; penitents have passed their lives in sack-cloth and ashes; martyrs have joyfully endured the most horrible torments. It is this science, in truth, which has enriched the Church in every age with righteous souls, and which continually peoples paradise with the souls of the just made perfect. Behold, then, the science which Jesus Christ teaches to His beloved, and which you, O devout soul, should use all diligence to acquire. Walk, then, in the light of this heavenly doctrine, and you too shall be numbered amongst the children of light.

Behold, most loving Jesus, prostrate at Thy

---

* Luke i. 79. † Philipp. iii. 20.

feet one who owns himself unworthy of the name of Thy disciple, but who desires, nevertheless, to be instructed by Thee in the science of the saints. " Speak, Lord, for Thy servant heareth." * Speak, Lord, and show me the way in which I ought to walk. Speak to me, and make me not only hear the words of eternal life, but relish them, love them and practise them. As Thou didst satisfy the soul of Magdalen with the sweetness of Thy heavenly discourse, so do Thou inebriate my soul also with the sweet unction of Thy Spirit. Ah! truly, all is vanity except to love Thee, my God, and to serve Thee alone. Pour forth, O Lord, into my heart a great horror of the false maxims of the world, and an intense delight in the maxims of the Holy Gospel. Take from me all love for things created; take Thou entire possession of my heart and soul. I trust to obtain grace through Thy infinite merits, O sweetest Jesus, and through thy intercession, O Mary, my most amiable Mother.

EJACULATION.—Teach me, O Lord, help me to become a saint.

---

* 1 Kings iii. 10.

Visit XVII.

In which we contemplate Jesus in the Blessed Sacrament as our Leader.

I. "*Behold I have given Him for a Leader and Master to the Gentiles.*"* One of the greatest privileges conferred by the Lord on the people of Israel during their pilgrimage through the wilderness was, that He sent His angel before them in a pillar of cloud to lead them during their long and perilous journey, and at length introduced them into the land of promise. This angel who guided the people of Israel was but a figure of the Son of God made Man, Jesus Christ our Lord, Who is called by Isaias the Angel of Good Counsel, and by Malachy the Angel of the Testament. With the tenderest care Jesus watches over us during our mortal pilgrimage, guiding us on our way, and leading us at length happily into our heavenly country. What lights and graces does He not diffuse within our souls by means of this Sacrament of love, and what strength does He not impart to us by this heavenly manna! Oh, what a touching spectacle would meet our gaze, were it given us to behold

---

* Isaias lv. 4.

unveiled, even for one moment, all that is contained in this sacred Host? We should see the heart of Jesus, like a burning furnace, inflamed with love for us, ever on the watch to shield us from dangers, and to arm us against our enemies, and to provide in a thousand ways for our salvation. Oh, thrice blessed are we, who possess in Jesus such a guide, who not only directs us in the path, but also feeds, sustains, and comforts us on the way, and conducts us safely to our heavenly home! Blessed are we, who have in Jesus such a guide, who can not only point out the dangers of the way, but also enable us to escape them! Blessed are we, who have in Jesus Christ a captain who first combats our enemies for us Himself, and places all His glory in conducting us triumphantly to the land of promise!

II. "*In all thy ways think on Him, and He will direct thy steps.*" * What does a blind man do who is so fortunate as to have a faithful guide? He abandons himself entirely into his hands, and allows himself to be directed as he wills. It is thus we ought to act with Jesus. What better guide can we desire than He? Let us then abandon ourselves entirely into His hands, and He will have care of us. "Cast thy care upon the

---

* Prov. iii. 6.

Lord, and He shall sustain thee." * Trusting ourselves to His guidance, we shall never err from the right way. "He that followeth Me," saith the Lord, "doth not walk in darkness, but shall have the light of life." † But woe to us, if we abandon such a Guide to follow the blind impulse of passion, which will most certainly prove our ruin. "If the blind lead the blind," says Jesus Christ, "both shall fall into the ditch." ‡

III. "*He that will come after Me, let him deny himself, and take up his cross daily, and follow Me.*" ‖ Behold, O devout soul, the great sentence which is inscribed in imperishable characters on the standard of Jesus Christ, our Leader. Let us not, then, deceive ourselves: if we would be of Christ's company, and have part with Him, we must before all things crucify self-love, resist our passions, and follow our great Captain, even to Calvary; but those weak souls who are sunk in softness and effeminacy, and prefer the flowery paths of the world to the thorny road of self-denial and of the cross, shall have no part with Christ, however great the toil and labour it may be their lot to meet with.

Turn then, most loving Jesus, one pitying

---

* Psalm liv. 23.
† John viii. 12. ‡ Matt. xv. 14.
‖ Luke ix. 23.

glance upon me, call me to take my place beneath Thy standard; I am resolved to follow Thee at any sacrifice, and to follow Thee to the end. "I will follow Thee whithersoever Thou goest." * Dispose of me as it seemeth good in Thy sight. I resign myself wholly to Thy sacred will. Suffice it for me to know that Thou lovest me. "Do as Thou wilt, dear Lord, with me......Enough that I am loved by Thee." Thou seest, far better than I can, all the needs of my soul. I trust myself entirely in Thy hands. Oh, conduct me to the portals of salvation. Like a lost sheep, I have wandered too long afar from Thee, my Shepherd. But, henceforth, my only desire is to be united to Thee for ever. Oh, strengthen by Thy grace the weakness of my resolves, and make me to become wholly Thine.

O Mary, my sweetest Mother, pray for me, obtain for me the grace to be faithful to your divine Son.

EJACULATION.—Have pity, Lord, on me, a wandering pilgrim upon earth, and guide me safely to my heavenly country.

Matt. viii. 19.

Visit XVIII.

In which we consider Jesus in the Blessed Sacrament as our Physician.

I. "*Jesus went about all Galilee......healing all manner of sickness and every infirmity amongst the people.*" * In reading the Gospel we are struck with astonishment at the great number of sick and diseased persons who were healed by our Lord. The lame, the blind, the deaf, the palsied, the lepers, the possessed —all, in fact, whatever their disease, found in Jesus Christ a Physician who relieved their infirmities and healed their sickness. But that which He did for their bodily ailments was but a figure of His operation on their souls, for He purged them from their sin, and healed them by His saving grace. How many came to Him with souls covered with wounds of sin, and returned from His presence pure as the infant just taken from the baptismal font! How many were so blessed as to hear from His sacred lips these words of peace, "Be of good heart, my son, thy sins are forgiven thee." † Reflect now, O devout soul, that this same Jesus,

---

* Matt. iv. 23. † Matt. ix. 2.

Who, in the days of His life on earth, succoured with such benignity man's weak and fallen state, is with us here unchanged upon our altars, and that the love which now burns within His sacred bosom is no less strong than that which consumed Him during His mortal sojourn amongst us. What may we not hope from His inestimable bounty? Ah, thrice happy are we, who can fly at any moment to our heavenly Physician, and be healed by Him of our spiritual maladies!

II. "*Those who are well have no need of a physician, but those who are sick.*" * Oh, ineffable goodness of our most loving Jesus! What more could He have done to animate our confidence, to encourage us to lay open our hearts to Him, to show Him our infirmities, and to beseech Him with loving confidence to heal them, than to assure us with His own lips that the physician is not for those who are well, but for the sick? Do not these words contain a most consoling invitation to fly to Him, whatever be the nature of our spiritual miseries, together with a most ample promise of healing them? Who, then, will be so foolish as to prefer rather to continue in his maladies, than to have recourse to this physician, so loving and so full of pity; to be content to bear the burden of his infirmities, rather

---

* Matt. ix. 12.

than to make use of the proffered medicine. "If thou didst know the gift of God."* Oh, if sinners did but know that unspeakable good which they might obtain by casting themselves with confidence into the arms of their divine Physician, earnestly beseeching Him to heal the wounds of their soul, without doubt men would hasten in crowds to prostrate themselves before His altar, and strive who should be first to receive from His hand the most excellent of gifts. But, alas for man's endless misery and degradation! fascinated by worldly pleasure, he knows but little of his true good, and therefore uses but slight endeavours to attain it.

III. "*Wilt thou be made whole?*" † Great as is the desire of Jesus to heal our infirmities, yet certain it is that He will not do so without our co-operation. As it was by our own will that we brought this disease upon our souls, so must our will co-operate with divine grace for our restoration. Do we, then, sincerely desire to be healed? Let us have recourse to our heavenly Physician. Whatever be the grievousness of our infirmity, even were it like that of the man sick of the palsy, who had lain for eight-and-thirty years in that severe state of affliction, yet will He receive us with benignity, and accord us that which we so

---
* John iv. 10.   † John v. 6.

much desire. But, if we have not this strong desire, and care not to beg it of God by means of prayer, it is certain that He will never free us from our evils. But how, O devout soul, do you correspond to the bounty of your divine Physician? Are you anxious to make use of the remedies which He prescribes? Are you in love with prayer and holy retirement? Do you frequent the sacraments devoutly? Do you endeavour to keep yourself as much as possible recollected in God? Do you study to purify your intention, and to keep a diligent guard over your heart, flying from all occasions of sin?

Ah, behold, dear Lord, he whom Thou lovest is sick.* Speak but one word, and my soul shall be healed. I deserve not that Thou shouldst heal me, it is true, but yet let Thy infinite mercy supply for my miserable unworthiness. Open Thou my eyes, that I may behold Thy light, and my ears that they may hear Thy voice; loosen my tongue, that it may hymn Thy eternal praises. Wash me, dear Lord, and make me clean from the leprosy of sin; quench the fire of concupiscence within me; deliver me from the fever of my passions. Chastise me as Thou wilt, but take not away Thy holy grace from me. Set free my heart from all earthly ties, and grant that I may

---

* John xi. 3.

live wholly for Thy love. Cause to descend upon me from above Thy heavenly fire, purifying my soul from every stain of earth.

O Mary, sweetest, gentlest of mothers, have pity on me, obtain this grace for me.

EJACULATION.—Wash me, O Lord, from my iniquities.

Visit XIX.

In which we contemplate Jesus in the Blessed Sacrament as our Shepherd.

I. "*I am the good Shepherd.*" * Amongst the various miseries to which men were subject before the coming of Christ, one was that "they were as sheep not having a shepherd." † But from the time Jesus Christ appeared amongst us, the state of things was changed, for man found in Him the true Shepherd, and one who far exceeded his expectations. Ah, happy indeed are we who live in these blessed days, wherein we have for our Shepherd the uncreated Wisdom of the Father Himself, the very Son of God made Man! What could we desire to find in a good shepherd that is not most perfectly realised in Jesus? Is He not continually on the watch to defend

---

* John x. 14. † Mark vi. 34.

us? Does He not provide with anxious care for our security? Where shall we find a shepherd who gives his own flesh for the food of his flock, and his own blood to be their drink, as Jesus does to us? And what shall we say of his love for His wandering sheep, and of His solicitude to lead them back to the fold? Who could have supposed that He would go in search of them Himself, and, having found them, would lay them on His shoulders rejoicing; that He would bear them back to the fold, and feel greater joy for the safety of the lost one than for all the rest of the flock that went not astray?* Oh, what tender charity! what excessive love!

II. "*The good Shepherd giveth His life for His sheep.*"† Who is this good Shepherd who giveth His life for His sheep, but our most loving Jesus, who gave His very life for our salvation? Ah, contemplate, O devout soul, your sweet Jesus fastened to the cross, His hands and feet transfixed by hard nails, His side pierced by a cruel lance; His head lacerated with the sharpest thorns; His face covered with blood; and His whole body one vast wound! What else but His love has reduced Him to this pitiable condition? His too great love for His sheep! From gazing on the cross, turn your eyes next upon this

---
* Luke xv. 5.   † John x. 11.

Sacrament of love, and behold our infinitely bountiful Jesus hidden beneath the Eucharistic veil, and become for us a perpetual victim. And what but love has reduced Him to such a state of unspeakable abasement and immolation—the exceeding love which He bears for His sheep? Yes, the Divine Shepherd of our souls sacrifices everything, He spares not even His life for us, who are unworthy to be called His sheep; and can we yet live without loving Him?

III. "*My sheep hear My voice, and I know them, and they follow Me.*" * To be worthy of being the sheep of this Divine Shepherd, it is not sufficient to belong externally to His fold; but we must meekly hearken to His voice, and faithfully follow His guidance. If we do not this, we may indeed deceive men and even delude ourselves, but we can have no part or lot with Christ. Even the very mark and character of His sheep, which was impressed upon our souls in Holy Baptism, will only add to our never-ending confusion and misery. Humble yourself, then, O devout soul, before the heavenly Shepherd, present yourself before Him as one of the sheep of His flock. Render Him thanks for having raised you to so high a dignity, and beseech Him never to permit you to become

---

* John x. 27.

unworthy of this grace. Tell Him that you desire no other pastures but those with which He feeds you in His heavenly doctrine and chiefly in the communion of His most sacred body. Implore Him to inflict upon you any chastisement, to send you any tribulation, rather than permit you to be separated even for a moment from Him.

Receive, dearest Lord, this soul of mine into the number of Thy flock. Give me grace to hearken meekly to Thy voice, and faithfully to follow after Thy sweet guidance. What are the pleasures of the world to me? What the praises of men but vanity and emptiness? I desire no other pasture than that which my beloved Jesus offers me. Oh, when shall I be able to love nothing but Thee, my dearest Saviour? When shall I be able to cling so closely to Thee that nothing may be able ever to separate me from Thy embrace? Why can I not leave this body and fly to Thy arms, my most beloved Lord? Oh, hasten the hour, the blessed hour, when Thou, my God, shalt perfectly reign in my soul, and I shall be wholly united to Thee. Grant me this favour, I beseech Thee, that I may be able very often to receive Thy sacred body, and to bathe my soul in Thy most precious blood. Behold, I renounce all things whatsoever, if I may but possess Thee, my most sweet Lord.

Remember me, O Mary, dearest of mothers. Make me worthy to be numbered in the flock of thy Divine Son.

EJACULATION.—Nourish, O Lord, my heart and soul with the unction of Thy Spirit.

VISIT XX.

In which we contemplate Jesus in the Blessed Sacrament as our Advocate.

I. "*My little children, these things I write to you that you may not sin. But if any man sin, we have an Advocate with the Father, Jesus Christ the just.*" * Oh, with what joy and confidence should our hearts be inspired at these most blessed words! What greater comfort can we have, when we most feel our weakness, than to know that Jesus Christ not only assists us that we may not fall, but even helps us to rise again when we fall, pleads our cause before His heavenly Father, obtains pardon for our sins, and admission once more to His favour? Where will the men of this world find such an advocate to plead their cause before the tribunals of their offended sovereign, whose favour they desire to recover? But that which cannot be found amongst men,

---

* 1 John ii. 1.

we find continually in our Saviour, Jesus Christ, Who, instead of repelling us when we have so grievously offended God, most graciously flies to our succour, and, if we will but permit Him to do so, undertakes our defence with His heavenly Father, propitiates His offended majesty, and restores us again to His grace. Ah, woe to those unhappy souls, who, possessing so easy a means of returning into the way of justice and of being reconciled with God, yet still continue in the abyss of sin, and in the end are lost. The very thought that they have thrown away such a means of salvation shall be for them a source of horrible torment for all eternity.

II. "*He is always living to make intercession for us.*" * The office of advocate, which our most loving Jesus exercises in our favour, is not restricted to any time, or to any one class of persons; it is perpetual, and regards all those who have recourse to Him, humbly imploring His grace. Carefully avoid sin, O devout soul. Sin is the greatest evil, or rather the only real evil which can befall you. But should you ever be so unhappy as to sin, oh, do not give way to any distrust of the mercy of your Advocate, but fly straightway to His holy presence, and, casting yourself before His holy Tabernacle, heartily implore

---

* Heb. vii. 25.

His gracious help, and He will most certainly hear you. Oh, how many sinners, oppressed by the enormous weight of their sins, have come hither, and prostrate before this throne of grace, humbly begging forgiveness, have found in Jesus their most merciful Advocate, who, coming promptly to their succour, has reconciled them with the outraged majesty of God.

III. "*Christ Jesus that died, yea, that is risen also again; Who is at the right hand of God, Who also maketh intercession for us.*" * Nothing so much torments some pious souls as the fear of being lost. What will become of us, say they, when we have to appear before the judgment-seat of God? Ah, peace, happy souls! for even then it is with your beloved Jesus you will have to treat. Let those indeed fear to fall into the hands of Jesus Christ, who obstinately continue in sin and abuse of His goodness. But those who earnestly desire to serve their Lord, and who, when they happen to fall, have immediate recourse to Him for succour, have no need to fear the moment in which they must appear in His presence; rather they have good cause to look forward to it with joy and confidence. For who is He that shall judge them? It is that same Jesus Who has given His life for them;

---

* Rom. viii. 34.

yea, who has risen again, who sits at the right hand of God, and who pleads their cause before His Heavenly Father.

Ah! my good Jesus, what would become of me, if my cause were to be judged according to the rigour of Thy justice? Well is it for me, indeed, that it depends on Thy mediation. I know full well that I deserve nothing but chastisement; yet, trusting in Thy infinite merits, I permit my heart to indulge in t' e most lively hopes in Thy goodness. If my sins threaten me with vengeance, Thy sacred wounds, Thy blood, Thy precious death, promise me pardon. If for my sins I have deserved death, yet Thou, my Jesus, hast merited life for me, even life eternal. Oh, when shall I see Thy face? When shall I behold Thy glory unveiled, and return Thee worthy thanks for all the care with which Thou hast sought my salvation? Oh, let me love Thee on earth, that so I may love and glorify Thee for ever in heaven.

Pray for me, Mary, my most sweet Mother, obtain for me this grace from thy dearest Son Jesus.

EJACULATION.—Grant me, O Lord, Thy holy grace for ever.

Visit XXI.

In which we contemplate Jesus Christ in the Blessed Sacrament as our High Prest.

I. "*We have a great High Priest......Jesus the Son of God.*" * The Israelites thought themselves most highly honoured in having in their midst the temple of the Lord, the priesthood, and the sacrifice. But far greater is our glory, O devout soul, in having with us Jesus Christ, the divine High Priest, who offers continually and in every place to His heavenly Father, not the blood of bulls and goats, but His own blood and His very life. Oh, stupendous mysteries, which we witness every day upon our altars, nothing less than the renewal and continuation of that same sacrifice which Jesus Christ once consummated on Mount Calvary; we behold our Lord offering that pure oblation of which the prophet Malachy foretold that it should be offered in every place, and that the name of God should become great amongst the Gentiles by its means. † We see, in fine, daily perpetuated amongst us the greatest of all the works of divine goodness.

II. "*Thou art a Priest for ever after the order of Melchisedech.*" ‡ The priests of the old

---

* Heb. iv. 14.
† Malachy i. 11.   ‡ Heb. v. 6.

law, besides being subject as men to infirmities and imperfections, and obliged to offer sacrifice for their own sins, were also mortal, and hence their priesthood was confined to the short span of their life on the earth. But far other is our divine High Priest, Jesus Christ, Who is innocent, undefiled, separated from sinners, and made higher than the heavens, Who needeth not daily (as our priests) to offer sacrifice first for His own sins and then for the people's. * For He, continuing for ever, hath an everlasting priesthood, whereby He is able also to save for ever them that come to God by Him. † Most blessed are we who can at every moment have recourse to this great High Priest, who is able at all times to lead us to God and to save us.

III. "*We have not a High Priest who cannot have compassion on our infirmities.*" ‡ With what confidence ought these most consoling words to fill our hearts! We have not a Priest, says the Apostle, who has no feeling for our infirmities; but one who has Himself shared all our miseries, sin only excepted. Yes, truly does Jesus Christ know to the very bottom all our wretchedness. He knows even by His own experience that we are but dust and ashes. He is not only very God, but true

---

* Heb. vii. 27.   † Heb. vii. 24.
‡ Heb. iv. 15.

and perfect Man ; and as Man He has Himself made trial of the weakness of our mortal nature. Who then shall express the boundless compassion and tenderness He feels for us His miserable creatures? Why does not the very thought of this make us as it were out of ourselves for joy? How is it that our hearts do not bound with feelings of the most lively joy, the most unbounded confidence in our dearest and most loving Jesus? What words can express our blessed lot? We have here within this sacred Tabernacle our divine High Priest, who cherishes in His heart at every moment sentiments of the most tender compassion for us, and offers up continually to His eternal Father His blood and His very life for our benefit. Ah, how often should we have fallen by reason of our sins beneath the heavy weight of the wrath of God, had not Jesus offered Himself for us to His Father a victim of propitiation, exhibited His wounds, and thus disarmed the divine justice, and obtained for us the grace of salutary penance! What things will on that day meet our view, when the veil which now conceals from us the secret working of divine bounty shall be withdrawn, and we shall behold all that Jesus Christ is now operating for our good!

O eternal and heavenly Father, I render Thee most hearty thanks for that Thou hast given to me this good High Priest, Jesus Christ Thy Son. How manifold are the ways of salvation which Thou hast opened to me, O God of infinite love! If I should, alas, miserably be lost, to what can I impute my failure but to my own inveterate malice? But, O my good God, this shall not be—I am resolved to avail myself of Thy goodness, to unite myself with Thy divine Son, my Redeemer, Jesus Christ. Oh yes, my dearest Jesus, I desire to love Thee, to love Thee for ever. Begone from me, false world, I hate and abhor thy deceits. Descend upon me, O heavenly fire of charity, come and inflame my heart with love. O my most loving Lord, give me a heart detached from all created things, and burning only with Thy holy love. This grace do I ask through the merits of Thy most sacred wounds, of Thy most precious blood. Oh, happy should I be could I say with Thy Apostle, "I live, now not I; but Christ liveth in me."*

O Mary, my well-beloved Mother, you who desired so much to see your dear Son Jesus loved by all, obtain for me the grace to live and to die for His holy love.

EJACULATION.—Thou, Lord, art the God of my heart and my portion for ever.

---
* Gal. ii. 20.

Visit XXII.

In which we contemplate Jesus in the Blessed Sacrament as our Guest.

1. "*My delight is to be with the children of men.*" * This earth is designed by Almighty God to furnish a temporary abode for those who live in passible and mortal flesh. As to those who have attained to an impassible and immortal life, He has assigned to them an everlasting habitation in the kingdom of eternal glory. What, then, shall we say when we behold Jesus, our most sweet Lord, not disdaining to dwell here within our churches and upon our altars, and even finding His delight in remaining amongst us? Ah, my good Jesus, what dost Thou behold in this miserable earth of ours, that Thou shouldst choose it for the place of Thy sojourn? Art not Thou indeed King of eternal glory? Is not Thy seat in heaven surrounded with resplendent light, and encompassed by myriads of saints and angels, who evermore pay Thee the tribute of their fervent homage? Why, then, dost Thou come to sojourn with us in this miserable valley of tears? Ah, my Jesus, I know full well the reason of this. Thou hast on

* Prov. viii. 31.

this earth objects most dear to Thy heart, objects which Thou dost love with a most ardent affection, and so Thou canst not remain afar from them, and deprive these beloved souls of Thy adorable Presence. Yes, dearest Jesus, our souls have been bought by Thee at the cost of Thy most precious blood, and have become through grace Thy beloved spouses, and do gentle violence to Thy heart, and move Thee to come amongst us and make Thyself our Guest.

II. "*I was a stranger, and ye took me in.*" * The love which Jesus Christ bears to us is shown not only by His dwelling within our churches and upon our altars, but still more by His entering into our very hearts, to unite our souls with Him by means of holy communion. Who could have believed in such an excess of charity, had he not himself beheld it? Is it not a subject of infinite astonishment, that the Son of God, the King of heaven and earth, should come to dwell within our souls, and that we, poor wretched worms, should have the honour of entertaining Him in our hearts? What should be our astonishment, our gratitude, our love, at being permitted to receive such a Guest? If St. Elizabeth was struck with awe at seeing the Mother of her God condescend to enter

---

* Matt. xxv. 35.

her humble dwelling, what ought to be our feelings when we behold Jesus Christ, true God and true Man, deign to unite Himself to us, and to enter within our very bosom?

III. "*Open to me, my love, my dove, my undefiled.*" * Oh, ineffable bounty of Jesus towards us, His miserable creatures! He is not satisfied to take up His abode amongst us, to be always at hand to communicate Himself to our souls; He even invites us to come to Him, and, as it were, entreats us to give Him a dwelling-place in our hearts. "I stand at the door of thy heart," says Jesus in the Sacrament of love, "and I knock: if any man then shall hear My voice, and open to Me the door, I will come in to him and will sup with him, and he with Me." † Oh, words of wondrous import! Man is so mean a thing in respect of God, that if he only knew his own profound baseness and the divine greatness, he would be wholly lost in the contemplation, and would never know how to humble himself enough in the sight of the divine majesty, not daring even to lift his eyes to heaven. What shall we say, then, when we behold this same infinite majesty not only abasing Himself so far as to dewll amongst us, miserable worms of the earth, and communicate Himself to our souls, but even

---

* Cant. v. 2. † Apoc. iii. 20.

earnestly longing to enter into our hearts, and entreating us to receive Him? What created mind, I say not of men, but even of angels, can comprehend such an infinite excess of love? Can we even think of it without being moved to tenderness, and our hearts being inflamed by the fire of Jesus' sacred charity? Can we remain insensible when we reflect on this stupendous, this ineffable prodigy of divine bounty? Jesus demands an entrance into our hearts, and we close the door upon Him, that we may give a ready entrance to sin.

O my Lord, soften by Thy grace this hardened heart, and melt it with the flame of Thy sweet charity. I am indeed most unworthy to receive Thee within my heart, but since Thou Thyself desirest to enter there, confiding in that same infinite bounty, I will approach to receive Thee as often as possible in Holy Communion, I will place all my delight in being constantly united with Thee. Come then, I beseech Thee, Jesus, my sweetest Lord, come and dwell within my soul, and make there Thy eternal resting-place. I desire nothing on this earth but to please Thee, and to enjoy without ceasing Thy adorable presence. Come into my soul, dear Lord, and enrich it with Thy graces. When Thou didst enter into the house of Zacchæus, Thou didst spread around Thy heavenly benediction:

Oh, do the same when Thou enterest the dwelling of my soul, speak to me as Thou didst then vouchsafe to speak: "This day is salvation come to this house."*

O Mary, Mother most dear, obtain for me the grace to make ready a dwelling worthy of Thy divine Son, that He may come and inflame me wholly with His sacred love.

EJACULATION.—Come, Lord, and sanctify my soul.

Visit XXIII.

In which we contemplate Jesus in the Blessed Sacrament as our Pattern.

I. "*Look and make all according to the pattern.*" † When the Lord commanded Moses to make the Tabernacle, He showed him first the model, and then told him to make all things according to the pattern He had shown him. Just as the Lord showed to Moses the pattern of the Tabernacle, so does He now continually present to us, in His only-begotten Son Jesus Christ, a divine form and model, commanding us to conform ourselves to Him, and to produce in our souls a copy as much

---

* Luke xix. 9. † Exod. xxv. 40.

like the original as possible. This is my beloved Son," God has declared from heaven, "in whom I am well pleased. If, then, you desire to have part in My love, and to obtain salvation, be sure that you clothe yourselves in His livery, that you imbibe His Spirit, that you follow His maxims, and copy His life. But, if you do not carry engraved on your soul the copy of this heavenly model, if I do not see there the likeness of My only begotten Son, I will certainly turn away from you as unworthy of My love, and meriting only My indignation.

II. "*Whom He foreknew, He also predestinated to be made conformable to the image of His Son.*"* Of what avail is it to us to be anxious about our future lot? Let us only endeavour to become like Jesus, and we shall certainly be saved. But, if we do not study to attain this conformity, then, indeed, may we tremble. Heaven is filled with saints of every sex, and age, and clime, of every condition and manner of education; but there is not one saint in heaven who is not perfectly conformed to the likeness of Jesus Christ. Hell is filled with the souls of the reprobate, for ever wailing in incessant torments: but, amidst all that multitude of reprobate beings, there is not one who

---

* Rom. viii. 29.

bears in his soul the slightest likeness to Jesus Christ. Let us not, then, deceive ourselves: Jesus Christ is the great model of the elect, to whom all who desire to be saved must conform themselves. If, at our departure from this world, our life is found conformable to His, the heavenly Father will recognise us as His own, and will call us into His eternal kingdom of bliss; but if, to our everlasting shame, we are found unlike this heavenly model, the divine Father will banish us for ever from His presence, and remove all His graces from us.

III. "*I have given you an example, that as I have done to you, so do you also.*"* Whom must we imitate? Our Saviour, Jesus Christ, is our model, O devout soul. He is our most loving Father, our most sweet Spouse; he walks securely who treads in His sacred footsteps. Whither does His example lead us, except to unite ourselves to God, and to gain eternal happiness in Him? At the hour of death what will it profit us to have followed the maxims and usages of the world, except to pierce our hearts with unavailing anguish, and to open to us the gates of eternal perdition? On the other hand, how great will be our consolation if we have remained throughout faithful to Jesus Christ,

---

* John xiii. 15.

and formed our lives after His example. Ah, truly, all is vanity except to unite ourselves to Jesus Christ, and to imitate Him alone. But, O devout soul, how do you endeavour to reproduce in yourself this divine model? Do you bear your cross with patience? Do you despise the world and its vanities? Do you keep your flesh under due restraint? Do you watch over your heart with all diligence? Do you wage continual war on your disorderly affections and vices? Are you detached from creatures? Is it your constant aim to do everything from the sole motive of pleasing God? Are you ready to suffer any pain, to make any sacrifice whatever, rather than offend God? In fine, do you love your Lord not in word only, but in deed and in truth?

I render Thee thanks, my dearest Lord, because Thou hast left me in Thy own life a model of all perfection and sanctity. It grieves me to my very heart that I have so often lost sight of this divine Model, living, as I have done, according to my own inclinations, and following my own caprice. Oh, by that love which moved Thee to give Thy life for me upon the cross, by that charity which induced Thee to take up Thy dwelling amongst us in this Sacrament of love, give me grace henceforth to detach my heart from all worldly vanity, and to think only of following Thy sacred footsteps, and of copying in my life Thy heavenly example. I renounce now and for ever the pleasures of this world; my only desire is to be united to Thee, and to conform as much as possible my life to Thine. Give me, dear Lord, I beseech Thee, to glory only in Thy cross, and to desire only to possess Thy holy love.

Pray for me, sweetest Mary, obtain for me the grace to conform my life in all things to that of Thy divine Son. I desire to love nothing but Jesus, and Jesus crucified.

EJACULATION.—O sweet Heart of my Jesus, make me to love Thee more and more.

Visit XXIV.

In which we contemplate Jesus in the Blessed Sacrament as our Food.

I. "*My Flesh is meat indeed, and my Blood is drink indeed.*" * Amongst the many prodigies which the Lord worked in favour of His ancient people during the pilgrimage to the land of promise, one of the greatest was that in which He provided them with food and drink, causing the manna to rain

---

* John vi. 56.

down from heaven, and streams to flow from the flinty rock. But far greater is that prodigy which He operates daily in our behalf, O devout soul, in providing us during the days of our pilgrimage to our heavenly country, not with corruptible food and drink, but with a heavenly and incorruptible bread, and a drink which never faileth, the very body and blood of His only-begotten Son, Jesus Christ. Who can comprehend the excess of love contained in this mystery of faith? Who could have believed that the love of Jesus Christ for us would lead Him even to give His own flesh for our nourishment, and for our drink His own most precious blood? Yes, that which it would have seemed almost madness even to imagine, we see daily before our eyes, and we have it in our power to partake of this Food as often as we will. "Take ye and eat," said this most loving Saviour to His disciples on that blessed night when He first instituted this Sacrament of love; "Take ye and eat, this is My body. — Take ye and drink, this is my blood."* Some may envy the happy lot of the apostles, who enjoyed in a visible manner the adorable presence of Jesus Christ. But far preferable is our happiness in having Him always present

---

* Matt. xxvi. 26.

with us in this divine Sacrament, and being able every day to receive Him into our hearts as the food and support of our souls.

II. "*He hath made a remembrance of His wonderful works, being a merciful and gracious Lord; He hath given food to them that fear Him.*" * Truly great are the marvels which the Lord works for our love, both in the order of nature and of grace. But the greatest of all these is the institution of the most Holy Eucharist, by means of which He becomes our food—Jesus Himself our spiritual nourishment. What greater treasure could He give us in this life than that which we have in this divine Sacrament? "Oh, wonder of wonders! Father Paul Segneri would exclaim after communion; "A God to me! a God to me!" And St. Mary Magdalen de Pazzi declared that a soul after communion might truly say, "It is finished." Jesus Christ, after communicating Himself to my soul, has no more to give me; He has in a manner exhausted all the treasures of His infinite riches.

III. "*Come ye and eat my bread, and drink the wine which I have mingled for you.*" † Great and costly was the feast which King Assuerus made for his nobles and the great men of his kingdom. But greater and more costly far is that feast which our divine

---

* Psalm cx. 4.   † Prov. ix. 5.

Saviour, the King of heaven and earth, continually makes for us in the most Holy Eucharist. That with which the table of Christ is provided, is no earthly and perishable food, but divine and heavenly; it is nothing less than His own most precious body and blood. Nor is this banquet spread only for some days or even years, but for all years and all time, even to the end of the world. The guests at this banquet are not the great ones of the earth, or the subjects of one nation only, but all Christians are called to partake of it, whatever their condition, or wheresoever they dwell. Whoever has the nuptial robe of charity is welcome to the table of Jesus Christ. But, O devout soul, how have you corresponded to this goodness which Jesus has shown you? What could He have done more to oblige us to love Him, than thus give Himself to us in this Holy Sacrament? And after this can you bear to live and not give yourself wholly to Him? Can you live any longer without consecrating your whole heart to His love? Jesus Christ invites you to feed upon His most sacred body, and can you dare to refuse His invitation, and to fill yourself with the filth of the earth? He constrains you to approach His table, and there partake of the food of life, and are you so blind as to keep aloof from Him, and to feed yourself with the bread of death?

Ah no, Jesus, my dearest Lord, never let me thus turn my back on Thy love. If, in times past, I have, alas! responded to Thy goodness only by ingratitude, I am now resolved to be wholly Thine. How blessed is my lot, to be thus permitted to feed upon Thy most sacred body! I renounce for ever the pleasures which the world offers to her votaries. I ask no other happiness than to unite myself with Thee, often to approach Thy table, and there to feed on that bread of life which is the delight and the support of the elect. Let others love and seek after earthly delights; for me, I will place all my happiness in loving Thee, my God. Yes, dearest Jesus, Thou shalt be for ever the God of my heart and my every Good. Confirm and strengthen by Thy grace my weak resolves, permit me not at any time to be separated from Thee.

And, O Mary, my sweetest Mother, to you I commend myself. I pray you to unite me closely to your Divine Son.

EJACULATION.—My Jesus, nourish my soul with Thy own most sacred body.

Visit XXV.

In which we contemplate Jesus in the Blessed Sacrament as our Life.

I. "*I am the Way, the Truth, and the Life.*" * Jesus is the Way, and we cannot otherwise reach our heavenly country than by following the path trodden by His sacred footsteps. He is the Truth, and we cannot otherwise obtain salvation than by following His holy maxims. He is, moreover, the Life, and in no other way can we gain the kingdom of glory than by living in Him and by Him. "I am the True Vine," He said to His disciples, "and my Father is the Husbandman; ......abide in Me and I in you. As the branch cannot bear fruit of itself, unless it abide in the vine, so neither can you, unless you abide in Me. I am the Vine, and ye are the branches; he that abideth in Me and I in him, the same beareth much fruit, for without Me you can do nothing." † Ah! why is it that men, who so eagerly desire life, do not unite themselves to Christ, who alone can give them life? Be not so miserably deceived. The goods which seem so tempting, and which

---

* John xiv. 6.   † John xv. 1, 4, 5.

you with so much ardour desire and seek after, far from being the source of life, only fill your heart with poisoned waters, and lead you to a miserable end.

II. "*The bread which I will give is my flesh for the life of the world.*" * Great indeed was the malice wherewith the devil sought to destroy mankind, but greater still is the goodness wherewith Jesus Christ seeks to save them. The devil despoiled our first parents of the supernatural life of grace, and plunged them with their posterity into an abyss of evil, when he persuaded them to eat the forbidden fruit. Jesus Christ, on the contrary, preserves and continually increases the spiritual life of grace in our souls, and replenishes them with every kind of good by the reception of His sacred body and His most precious blood. "The bread which I will give," says Jesus from the sacred Tabernacle, "is My flesh for the life of the world. The people of Israel did eat manna in the desert and are dead; he that eateth this bread shall not die for ever. As the Father hath sent Me, and I live by the Father, even so he that eateth Me, shall live by Me. My flesh is meat indeed, and My blood is drink indeed. If ye eat not the flesh of the Son of Man, and drink not His blood, ye shall have no

---

* John vi. 52.

life in you. He that eateth my flesh and drinketh my blood, hath eternal life, and I will raise him up at the last day." Who then will be so cruel towards his own soul as to choose to nourish himself with filth and ordure, when he may have for his portion the food of Paradise? Who so blind as to give himself up a prey to death, when he might eat the bread of eternal life at will?

III. "*They have left Me, the fountain of living water, and have dug for themselves broken cisterns.*" * They who turn their back upon the fountain of life, and dig for themselves impure and broken cisterns, are those who abandon Christ to live after the dictates of their own miserable passions. What madness! What blindness of heart! What more could they have done, if instead of eternal life eternal death were to be their end? Ah, would that their number were but small! would that few might incur this terrible ruin! but, alas! these miserable beings abound on all sides; and thus, accursed world, thou ruinest so many poor souls, created to live eternally with Christ in heaven.

Behold me prostrate at Thy feet, my dearest Jesus. I adore Thee as the Author of my life. I render Thee heartfelt thanks for all Thy numberless benefits, but more especially

---

* Jer. ii. 13.

because Thou hast borne with me so patiently whilst I have been walking in the way of perdition, and hast now given me grace again to enter into the way of life. Where should I now be, hadst Thou taken me out of this world when I was Thy enemy? Ah! I should long since have been in the kingdom of eternal death, and condemned everlastingly to those dismal regions. For ever blessed be Thy infinite goodness, which has thus borne with me, and again conducted me back into the path of safety. Oh, permit not, I beseech Thee, dearest Lord, that I should ever again fall into that dreadful state of shame and ruin. I desire nothing but Thy love; to be united inseparably to Thee; and to be Thine wholly and for ever. What have I to do with worldly satisfactions and delights? Thou only, my Jesus, art my true delight, my happiness, my glory, and my every good. Come then, dear Jesus, into this soul of mine, visit me often by Thy grace, give me to live a divine life in Thee.

I fly to Thy patronage, O holiest and sweetest Mother, preserve my soul from eternal death.

EJACULATION. — O Jesus, Life of my soul, guide me to the mansions of the blest who live in Thee.

Visit XXVI.

In which we contemplate Jesus Christ in the Blessed Sacrament as our Comforter.

I. "*His conversation hath no bitterness, nor His company any tediousness, but joy and gladness.*" * Although Jesus Christ allows souls beloved by Him to be tried by many and grievous crosses, yet He fails not to relieve them in their afflictions, and to make them taste from time to time the dew of His heavenly consolation. How great is the sweetness, O Lord, which Thou hast prepared for those that fear Thee, † said the prophet David. In the world, where men delight only in the pleasures of sense, it is scarcely believed that souls which love God and fear the least defilement of sin more than death itself can enjoy any real pleasure whatever. But what would be the astonishment of worldlings if it were given them to see the interior of these souls, and to behold the calm sweetness, peace and joy which their heavenly Spouse in the midst of all their crosses bestows upon them! Ah no, to converse with God is no cause of sadness;

---

* Wisd. vii. 16.   † Psalm xxx. 20.

nor does communion with Him bring with it weariness and satiety; here on the contrary is the very source of all happiness and joy.

II. "*Come unto Me all ye that labour and are heavy burdened, and I will refresh you.*" * Who is it that thus sweetly invites us, and makes this most consoling promise? Who is it that calls us to Him, that He may comfort us in our tribulation and relieve our afflictions? Is it some great sovereign of this earth, or an angel of heaven? Ah, for ever praised and blessed be the infinite bounty of our most loving Saviour! How consoling to us should be the thought that in this our miserable exile, in this valley of tears, in the tempestuous sea of life, we have ever with us Jesus Christ, the God of all consolation, and that we can always have recourse to Him, and be relieved by Him in all our miseries. Are our tribulations great and our afflictions heavy upon us? Let us fly with confidence to the throne of grace, and Jesus, our sweetest Jesus, will take pity on us and comfort us. "Come unto me," saith Jesus, from yonder sacred tabernacle, "draw near to me all ye that are oppressed, are burdened, are afflicted, and I will comfort you, I will console you, I will give you rest. I have here the medicine which heals every disease. Come, then, to My bosom, and I will heal your

---

* Matt. xi. 28.

wounds; come to My heart, and I will pour into your soul the sweet balsam of my consolation."

III. "*O taste and see that the Lord is sweet.*" * What fruit do worldlings draw from earthly pleasures? Alas! unhappy souls, instead of deriving from them the satisfaction they expect, they find in the end nothing but bitterness and affliction of spirit. Far different is the lot of those who love God; they find in Jesus the source of all their consolation. "Happy, thrice happy day," exclaimed St. Austin, "when I turned to thee, O ancient Beauty ever new, when I emptied my heart of the false delights of this world, and Thou didst enter there instead, and didst spread abroad a sweetness which knows no equal. O ye men who groan under the oppressive burden of this world's miseries, why do you not fly to the fountain of every good? Why do you not seek comfort from Jesus? Ah, leave once and for ever the ways of sin; cast yourself into Jesus' arms; unite yourself to Him, and you shall quickly perceive the sweetness, the consolation which He will infuse into your heart. Approach His table, take His flesh for your nourishment, and therein you shall find the remedy of all your ills. For the food with which that table is spread is the Food of Paradise,

---

* Psalm xxxiii. 9.

which exceeds in sweetness all the choicest delights this world can afford." "No tongue," says St. Thomas, "can express the sweetness of that Divine Sacrament. Enough that there we drink of sweetness in its very source."

How lovely are Thy tabernacles, O Lord of hosts! My soul longeth and fainteth for the courts of the Lord. My heart and my flesh have rejoiced in the Living God. Thy altars, O Lord, are Thy throne, my King and my God.* Blessed are they that dwell in Thy house, O Lord: they shall praise Thee for ever and ever. Far better is one day spent in Thy house, than thousands in the tents of the impious. I have chosen to be an abject in the house of my God, rather than to dwell in the tabernacles of sinners. Turn into bitterness, I beseech Thee, O Lord, every earthly delight; make me to desire no other pleasure than to love Thee with my whole heart. O Thou, who art the Comforter of the afflicted, the Consoler of the sorrowful, pour upon my soul the unction of Thy Spirit, fill my soul with a holy peace and calm. I ask this grace of Thee, through the merits of Thy most holy wounds, of Thy most bitter passion. Vouchsafe to me one look of compassion.

Mary, my Mother and most sweet advocate,

---

* Psalm lxxxiii.

obtain for me the grace evermore to love thy divine Son.

EJACULATION. — O Jesus, comforter of the sorrowful, relieve my soul in its affliction.

VISIT XXVII.

In which we contemplate Jesus in the Blessed Sacrament as our Sanctifier.

I. "*Christ loved the Church, and delivered Himself up for it, that He might sanctify it.*" * Wherefore did Jesus permit Himself to be nailed like a malefactor to the cross, rendering up His life amidst a sea of torments? Wherefore does He continue still to offer upon our altars this great sacrifice to His Eternal Father? Why does He remain within this sacred Tabernacle, and there receive us into His presence with such unspeakable benignity? Why does that sacred heart so burn to communicate Itself to us? Ah, if Christians only knew the reason of this, doubtless they would desire their sanctification far more earnestly than they do at present. The great object which the heart of Jesus ever had in view in all He did and suffered, was our sanctification. Christ loved

---

* Eph. v. 25, 26.

His Church, says the Apostle, and offered Himself up for its sanctification. He gave Himself for us, that He might redeem us from all iniquity, and might cleanse to Himself a people acceptable, a pursuer of good works.* Oh, marvellous inventions of charity! Shall we esteem our sanctification so little as to neglect it for the false joys of this earth? Jesus Christ, true God and true Man, sacrificed Himself for us, and thought His blood and life well spent for our salvation; and yet we regard Him with indifference, and we think it too much to renounce our passions, to sacrifice our disorderly affections, and even use every effort to gratify them. Jesus Christ dwells continually with us, and communicates Himself to our souls, to sanctify them; and we live, alas! forgetful of our sanctification, and wholly given up to the vanities of this world.

II. "*Jesus Christ, Who of God is made unto us Wisdom, and Justice, and Sanctification.*" † Jesus Christ works our sanctification in many ways, but chiefly by means of the most Holy Eucharist. Whence did the early Christians draw that fervour of charity which astounded even their enemies, if not from frequent and daily participation of this Sacrament of love? ‡ Whence did the Martyrs

---

* Tit. ii 14.

† 1 Cor. i. 30.   ‡ Acts ii. 42.

draw that heroic faith and courage which filled their persecutors with wonder, but from this food of Paradise, which they received to prepare themselves for martyrdom? Where does Jesus Christ diffuse the heavenly fire of His love in greatest measure? Is it not in this divine Sacrament, wherein He resides in person, and communicates Himself most intimately to our souls? What souls have ever approached devoutly to that heavenly table, and have not returned from it renewed in spirit and replenished with strength to tread the path of sanctity? We read that the prophet Elias, having eaten of the bread brought to him by the hand of the angel, felt himself so invigorated that he continued his journey for forty days and nights to the top of the mountain of the Lord. "He went on the strength of that food......to Horeb, the mount of God."* That which befel the prophet Elias was only a figure of what happens continually to so many Christians who partake worthily of this heavenly food, and who are able, in the strength which they here receive, to ascend with ease the mountain of perfection. How blessed, then, is our lot, who have continually with us in this divine Sacrament a source of inexhaustible light, strength, and holiness!

---

* 3 Kings xix. 8.

III. "*Be ye holy, because I am holy.*" *
Behold, O devout soul, what your most loving Jesus expects at your hands. He expects you to co-operate faithfully with His graces, to correspond with His bounty, and to attend seriously to the great work of your own sanctification. As He Himself is holy, so does He desire that souls beloved by Him should strive with earnestness to attain to holiness. And what are we aiming at if we are not really desirous of becoming Saints? What would it profit us to gain the whole world, if we should be eternally lost? Truly, all is vanity and illusion, except to love God and serve Him alone. Let us, then, cast off our tepidity, let us rouse ourselves to holy fervour, let us consecrate ourselves to the love of Jesus Christ. Do we suppose that those souls which have attained the highest pitch of sanctity were perfect from the first? No, truly; they were once as weak and imperfect as we are ourselves, but, little by little, Jesus in the Blessed Sacrament drew them to to Himself, and made them saints. What then hinders us from becoming saints? "If these were able, who were weak men and women, like ourselves," as St. Augustine would say, "what hinders me?" Have we not on our altars the same Jesus who formed the

---

* Levit. xi. 44.

delight of their hearts? And is He not ever ready to communicate to us the same graces which He imparted to them? Can we not fly to Him, unite ourselves to Him, and receive Him frequently into our breasts, as they did? Ah, woe to us, if, instead of following them in the way of sanctity, we allow ourselves to be overcome by our own tepidity and sloth!

I render Thee eternal thanks, most loving Jesus, for Thy infinite bounty in suffering so many pains, and working such marvels for our sanctification. Oh, how does it grieve me that I have hitherto corresponded so ill with such unspeakable graces! But now I am resolved to direct all my efforts to become a saint. Draw me, dear Lord, to Thee, and inflame me with Thy holy love. As the hart panteth after the fountains of water, so longeth my soul after Thee, O God,* my only Good. Let others have the goods of this earth; for me, I have no desire but to unite myself most closely with Jesus, and to be His own for ever. Pour forth into my soul, dear Lord, Thy divine Spirit: make me a perfect victim of Thy love. Happy should I be, could I detach myself wholly and for ever from all things of this earth, to attend only to the love of my God.

O Mary, my sweetest Mother, pray for me

---

* Psalm xli. 2.

obtain for me the grace to live and to die, loving only Thy dearest Son Jesus Christ.

EJACULATION.—O Jesus, Sanctifier of souls, sanctify this soul of mine.

VISIT XXVIII.

In which we contemplate Jesus in the Blessed Sacrament as our Judge.

I. "*It is He who was appointed by God to be Judge of the living and dead.*" * Jesus Christ remains at present on our altars hidden beneath the Eucharistic species, and intent only on pouring forth upon us the treasures of His grace. But the day will come when He will draw aside the veil which now conceals Him from our sight, and will present Himself to our eyes, refulgent with excess of light, in all the brightness of His glory. "They shall see the Son of Man," as He Himself declares, "coming in the clouds with great power and majesty." † On that day we shall behold Him descending from the highest heavens, seated on a white and shining cloud, full of majesty and glory, surrounded by myriads of angels and of saints, coming to judge all the nations of the earth. Now He inspires no other feelings

---

* Acts x. 42. † Luke xxi 27.

than those of sweetness and tenderness; but then His presence will strike us with fear and trembling. Now He shows forth only the kingdom of His mercy; but then the day of His justice will have come. For "then shall He render to every man according to His works." *

II. "*We must all be manifested before the judgment-seat of Christ, that every one may receive the proper things of the body, according as he hath done, whether it be good or evil.*" †

How can we reflect on these words without feeling in our hearts a deep contempt of all the things of this earth, and a most lively desire of becoming saints? What a spectacle will that day disclose! As we have been redeemed by the blood of Christ, so must we appear one day before His tribunal to answer for the use or the abuse we have made of His most sacred blood, shed for us. Whatever be the road in which we are walking on this earth, we must at last arrive before the judgment-seat of Christ, we must meet the piercing eye of the all-seeing Judge, and give an account of all the good or evil we have done, and hear from His divine lips the tremendous sentence which will decide our lot for all eternity. O my God, what will then become of us? Shall we be found on Thy right hand

---
* Rom. ii. 6. † 2 Cor. v. 10.

or on Thy left? Shall we have place among the spotless lambs of Jesus Christ, or shall we be numbered amongst the outcast goats of Satan? Shall we be associated to the glorious army of the elect, or the infamous multitude of the reprobate? Shall we behold Jesus Christ with eyes of tenderness and love, or with horror and despair? Shall we hear from his lips the sentence of salvation or of condemnation? What would be our fate were we at this moment presented before that terrible tribunal? What if Jesus were now to draw aside the veil wherewith He conceals Himself in this Sacrament of love, and from being our most tender Advocate become at once our Almighty Judge? Who could then absolve us, if He should condemn us? Oh, if our conscience tells us that we should then be condemned, let us lose no time, but instantly set our hand to the work of saving our soul! What pains should we not take to secure the prosperous issue of a law-suit on which our honour, our fortune, or our life might depend! And are we, then, only negligent when there is question of securing a happy issue to that dread sentence on which our eternal salvation or misery depends? Oh, let us profit by the goodness of Jesus Christ, while yet He gives us time; let us walk in the light while yet it shines upon us; let us not wait till the time of darkness has come. It is yet in our power to choose whether we will be found on the right hand or the left of the Judge; let us unite ourselves closely to Jesus, and all shall be well. But in that tremendous day this will not be in our power; it will then be too late when we shall be called before the dread tribunal. Then mercy will be silent, and justice only will be heard. Then happy will he be who has done good in his lifetime; but misery and damnation shall be the portion of the wicked.

III. "*Behold the Judge standeth before the door.*" * When shall we be called to appear before Christ's judgment-seat? When shall we be carried before His terrible tribunal? Let us be always ready, for that tremendous day may surprise us at any instant. "Be ye ready," saith Jesus Christ, "for at what hour you think not the Son of Man will come." † "I will come to thee as a thief, and thou shalt not know at what hour I will come to thee." ‡ "Blessed is that servant, whom His Lord when He cometh shall find watching."

Behold me, dearest Lord, prostrate at Thy feet. I am unworthy to be called Thy son, yet it grieves me to my heart that I have

---

* James v. 9.
† Luke xii. 40.   ‡ Apoc. iii. 3.

offended Thee; most humbly I implore Thy pardon. Oh, deal not with me after the measure of my offences, but according to the multitude of Thy mercies. Grant me pardon of my sins before the day of vengeance comes, and give me grace to love Thee above all things. Remember, I beseech Thee, that if Thou shalt hereafter be my judge, Thou art now my most amiable Saviour and most beloved Spouse. Remember that I am the work of Thy hands, the price of Thy blood. Turn upon me Thy most pitying eyes, look upon me as Thou didst look upon the penitent Magdalen, and save me. Thrice blessed shall I be if on that great and terrible day, when Thou shalt come to judge all nations of the earth, I shall be found amongst the elect on Thy right hand, to enjoy the sweetness of Thy countenance, and listen to the words of grace which proceed from Thy most sacred lips! Afflict me now as Thou wilt, chastise me in this life, but permit me not to lose Thee for eternity.

Mary, my sweetest Mother, have compassion on me; recommend me to thy Son.

EJACULATION.—O Jesus, may I find Thee sweet and merciful when Thou shalt come to judge my soul.

Visit XXIX.

In which we contemplate Jesus in the Blessed Sacrament as our Glorifier.

I. "*To him that shall overcome, I will give to sit with me on My throne: as I also have overcome, and am sat down with My Father on His throne.*" * Our life on this earth is a continual warfare. † Who can count the enemies that surround us, and their manifold assaults upon us? On one side we have the infernal spirits using every endeavour to make us sin, and to render us subject to their power; again we have the world, which leaves nothing untried to corrupt our heart and enslave it to its own false maxims. Here we are assaulted by the flesh, lying in wait to seduce us with its deceitful baits, and to draw us into the abyss of crime; there our own self-love does all it can to separate us from God, and to make us live after the desires of our own passions. We find ourselves, in fine, as in a field of battle, surrounded on every side by enemies. Yet let us not be cast down, but

---

* Apoc. iii. 21.   † Job vii. 1.

rather rejoice and take fresh courage, since, if we fight with valour the battles of the Lord, we shall without doubt receive the crown of victory. Let us rejoice, because Jesus, Who is now our Leader, will bring us at length into His kingdom in triumph, and will make us sit with Him on a throne of glory for endless ages. Let us rejoice, knowing that if we follow Jesus now in the way of humiliation, we shall also follow Him into the place of His triumph; if we are companions of His pains, we shall be also of His consolation; if we partake of His sufferings, we shall in like manner partake of His glory. "The world shall rejoice, but you shall be sorrowful," He says to us from the holy Tabernacle,—" but your sorrow shall be turned into joy." * Now you weep, but the day will come when He shall wipe away all tears from your eyes, and there shall be no more weeping, but you shall rejoice for an endless eternity. Now, indeed, you groan beneath the weight of a fragile and mortal body, but the day will come in which He shall re-form this body, communicating to it a ray of His own effulgence, whereby it shall shine like the sun in its strength; "for this corruptible must put on incorruption, and this mortal must put on immortality." †

"To him that overcometh," says our sweet

---

* John xvi. 20. † 1 Cor. xv. 53.

Jesus, "I will give to eat of the fruit of the tree of life. To him will I give the hidden manna, which no man knoweth but he that receiveth it. He that overcometh shall be clothed in white, and I will confess his name before God and His angels. Him that overcometh I will make to become a pillar in the temple of my God. I will make him to sit with Me upon my throne, even as I also have overcome, and am sat down on my Father's throne." * Why are we not wholly inflamed with sacred fervour at these holy words? Do we not feel a new ardour enkindled within us to fight valiantly against our enemies? What matters it if the combat be long and arduous, when our fidelity will be so amply rewarded? What are all our present sufferings when compared with the joy which shall hereafter be given us? Let us then for a while sustain the fight, for after the battle comes the victory. Let us bear patiently the momentary tribulations of this life, and we shall quickly be repaid by an eternal weight of glory in heaven. †

II. "*I am thy reward exceeding great.*" ‡ What would be our emotions of joy and love, if it were given us to behold unveiled Jesus Christ hidden in this Adorable Sacrament! If the

---

* Apoc. ii. 17 ; iii. 5, 12, 21.
† 2 Cor. iv. 17.   ‡ Genes. xv. 1.

three disciples who were present at the Transfiguration were ravished out of themselves when they beheld in part only the splendour of His body, what would be our transports could we fix our eyes, not on the body only, but on the most holy soul of Christ, and on His Divinity Itself, and admire all the splendours of that ineffable glory? If some souls have not known how to contain themselves for the joy they felt in contemplating the perfections of their Spouse, seen by them only with the eyes of faith, what excess of joy would be ours, were it given us to behold Him face to face in the full splendour of His glory? What would be the transport of our heart at the sight of such unspeakable beauty and perfection? What would be our astonishment and wonder at the sight of that throne of purest light, on which He sits surrounded by angels and saints, who form His crown? Oh, joy beyond conception great! glory exceeding man's imagination to conceive! an immortal crown prepared by Jesus Christ for all His faithful soldiers! a reward beyond all price prepared for souls beloved by Him! Ah, happy and blest will be our lot, if we shall have fought His battles with fidelity, for He Himself will be our eternal reward!

III. *"He that striveth for the mastery, is*

not crowned except he strive lawfully." * Glorious is the lot of those who fight valiantly beneath the standard of Christ! After a brief contest they shall enter for ever into the joy of their Lord, they shall shine like stars for all eternity, and shall be for ever inebriated with the plenty of their Lord's house. † What tongue can tell, what intellect can comprehend, the bliss of being admitted to the Divine Presence, together with all the choirs of angels, to hymn the Creator's glory, to behold unveiled the face of God, and to be wholly consummated with Him in charity! Truly, eye hath not seen, nor ear heard, neither hath it entered into the heart of man to conceive the delights which God hath prepared for those that love Him. ‡ But reflect well, O devout soul, that if we would be crowned with Christ hereafter, it is absolutely necessary that we now combat valiantly with Him against His and our enemies. He only that fighteth shall gain the victory, and he only that is victorious shall be crowned. If, then, the greatness of the reward allures us, which Christ has prepared for His faithful soldiers, let not the fatigues of the combat discourage us, since great rewards are never gained but through great labour and toil. But if, instead of fighting, we lay down our arms

---

* 2 Tim. ii. 5.

† Ps. xxxv. 9. ‡ 1 Cor. ii. 9.

and fly from the combat, we shall be far from having any part with Christ, we shall be repelled by Him as unworthy of His love, and shall be cast with the unprofitable servant in the gospel into the exterior darkness, where there shall be weeping and gnashing of teeth. *

I thank Thee, my dearest Lord Jesus, for Thy goodness in calling me to bear part in Thy blessed kingdom, and admitting me to share in the glory of Thy faithful followers. Oh, purify my soul from every stain, make it worthy of that blessed country, where nothing defiled can enter. How blest would be my lot, if at the end of my life I might breathe out my soul in Thy sacred arms, and be by Thee introduced into the blessed regions of Paradise! Oh, may Thy kingdom quickly come! Would that the day were here, when the members shall be united to their Head, the children to their Father, the subjects to their King, the sheep to their most tender Shepherd,—that day of clearness and of light, when all darkness shall pass away; of mercy and of grace, when all the heavenly treasures shall be disclosed; of joy and exultation, when our hearts shall be immersed in the sea of the eternal enjoyment of God!

Trusting in Thy wounds and in Thy sacred blood, I hope, most loving Saviour, that Thou

* Matt. xxv. 30.

wilt pardon my sins and admit me to the possession of Thy glory. Hence I am resolved to walk in Thy footsteps, to imitate Thy blessed example, to embrace Thy cross, to die to all created things, in order to live only to Thee, and to reign with Thee eternally in heaven.

. O Mary, Queen of heaven, pray to thy divine Son Jesus for me, obtain me the grace to praise, to thank, to love Him with thee for ever in Paradise.

EJACULATION.—Come, O sweet Jesus, reign wholly in this heart of mine.

Visit XXX.

In which we contemplate Jesus in the Blessed Sacrament as our All.

I. "*I am, who am.*"* All created beings, how high soever their dignity and prerogatives, not excluding the most exalted Seraphim, possess only a limited and finite good, which, moreover, they have not of themselves, for they have received all from the hands of God. But Jesus Christ, being very God, possesses in Himself an unlimited and infinite good, contains within Himself every good; and this belongs to Him of His own nature

---

* Ex. iii. 14.

without His being indebted for it to any other being. Hence He is truly that which He is, namely, Essential Good, Author of all good. Let us conceive any kind of perfection, let us represent to our mind whatever excellence we please; it is certain that all this is possessed by Jesus Christ in an infinite degree. Moreover, all the perfection and excellence of all the creatures which fill heaven and earth, are, as it were, but a faint ray of that one infinite Goodness and Beauty. What then shall we say of those Christians who seek for good apart from Jesus Christ? "Ah, deluded beings," says St. Augustine, "whither do you go to seek for goods of soul and body? Seek that One Good, in whom is every good!"

II. "*I am Alpha and Omega, the Beginning and the End.*"* The world promises to its followers satisfactions, delights, and every kind of good. But how does it fulfil its promises? Alas! the world is a traitor which, whilst it seduces us on the one side with its deceits, aims on the other a mortal blow at our hearts. It has succeeded up to this time in making an infinite number of beings miserable, but has not yet been able to make a single being happy. Its false promises may deceive us with the appearance of good, but they can never satisfy us. Where then shall we find

---

* Apoc. i. 8.

a good which can fully satisfy our longings, and fill the vast capacity of our hearts? Lift up your eyes, O devout soul, and fix them on yonder altar, on yonder sacred Tabernacle, and there you will find your Treasure and your every good. Jesus, your most loving Jesus, who here treats with you so tenderly in the Divine Sacrament, is your Beginning, your End, your every Good. What can be wanting to Him, who possesses the King of heaven and earth, the God of majesty and glory, the Source of all blessedness; in fine, an infinite and endless Good? What tenderness of love ought we not to conceive towards our most loving Jesus at this consideration! So deeply was St. Francis of Assisium impressed with this thought, that he passed whole nights in loving converse with his Lord, repeating again and again, these words "My God and my All, my God and my All." Ah, happy should we be could we truly penetrate what these words signify, and feel their force in our inmost soul!

III. "*If God be for us, who is against us?*"* Let us keep close to Jesus, and we have nothing to fear. What have we to fear if Jesus Christ be with us? Has He not sovereign power in heaven and earth? Does He not hold in His hands the hearts of

---

* Rom. viii. 31.

all men? Does He not direct all events for the good of His elect? Why then should we fear, if He be with us? Shall we fear the tribulations of this life? No, for these Jesus can so sweeten by His grace, that they shall turn to our endless triumph. Is it death we have to fear? No, for Jesus has overcome death and taken away all its terrors, making it become sweet and peaceful to the souls that love Him. Let us then love Jesus, and be sure that were all creatures to rise up against us, they would not be able to hurt us; for, with all their efforts to injure us, they would co-operate for our good, and increase our crown. Let us keep ourselves united to Jesus, and say with the prophet David, "The Lord is my light and my salvation, whom then shall I fear? The Lord is the protector of my life, of whom shall I be afraid? If armies in camp should stand together against me, my heart shall not fear. If a battle should rise up against me, in this will I be confident." *

Alas! what blindness have I shown in having hitherto put my trust in creatures, rather than in Thee, my dearest Lord, my Creator, and my every Good. It grieves my inmost soul thus to have abused Thy bounty. But yet have mercy, Lord, on me a wretched sinner,

---

* Ps. xxv. 1-3.

grant me pardon of all my faults. Give me grace to repair the offences I have committed against Thee, by loving Thee without limit for the time to come, and dedicating what yet remains of 'this life of mine entirely to Thy holy service. I renounce all earthly satisfactions, and desire nothing but to give Thee what is justly due from me, my God, my treasure, and my every good. My heart sighs for Thee alone, in Thee I place all my trust, Thou art my only good. Draw me, dear Jesus, with the chains of Thy love, bind me close to Thy heart, inebriate me with Thy charity, give me Thy love with Thy grace, and I am rich enough, and I wish and seek for nothing more; Thou shalt be the God of my heart, and my portion for ever.

O Mary, my hope and my sweet refuge, I fly to Thy protection, let me never cease to love Thy dearest Son Jesus.

EJACULATION.—O my God, and my every good.

Visit XXXI.

In which we contemplate Jesus Christ as our Victim.

I. "*Greater love than this no man hath, that a man lay down his life for his friends.*" * The whole of the tenth chapter of St. Paul's Epistle to the Hebrews is directed to showing that one only sacrifice or host was substituted for the many sacrifices of the Old Testament, that host being Our Lord Jesus Christ: "Offering one sacrifice (host) for sins." † This one host, and not many hosts, we offer daily on our altars in the sacrifice of the Eucharist! "O Salutaris Hostia!" ‡ Although then everything offered to God in sacrifice may be called a host or victim, § yet only the Eucharist is called the Sacred Host, because it is the only victim offered to God in expiation of the sins of the whole world, and for the same reason it is called in the Canon of the Mass, "A pure host, a sacred host, a spotless host."

Jesus Christ gives Himself to us in the

---
* John xv. 13.   † Heb. x. 12.
‡ St. Thomas Aq. "Verbum Supernum.'
Rom. xii 1; Heb. viii. 3; xiii. 15, 16; 1 Pet. ii. 5.

Holy Eucharist immolated, as it were, and with His blood separated in the only manner possible from His body, for He says: "This is my body;" and then: "This is my blood;" and thus He lays Himself on the altar a Host of immolation for us, in the same way as He delivered His body to death and shed His blood: "This is my body which is delivered up for you." "This is my blood......which shall be shed for you." * No longer shadows and figures! The Lord is weary now of the smoke of sacrifice, of the fat of sheep and of oxen; He takes pleasure only in the Sacred Host of our altars.

> Here for empty shadows fled
> Is reality instead;
> Here, instead of darkness, light. †

Oh, who will give me to be more and more united with that blessed body sacrificed for me, who will give me to plunge into that blood which cleanses from all sin! "O Salutaris Hostia!"

II. "*Blessed are they that have washed their robes in the blood of the Lamb.*" ‡ To be victims of charity like Jesus Christ is the high vocation of all the elect, for, as the

---

* Luke xxii. 19, 20.
† St. Thomas Aq. "Lauda Sion."
‡ Apoc. xxii. 14.

sacrifice of the cross was perpetuated in the martyrs in the primitive ages, so subsequently and at the present time it is continued in the countless victims of charity who immolate themselves in a thousand ways for the love of God and of their neighbour, strengthened by the virtue of the Eucharistic sacrifice. Every holy soul is a victim of charity. The Eternal Father sent His only begotten Son into this world to be immolated for our sins, and Jesus Christ desires that His followers should also become victims of divine love. For He says, "I am come to bring fire on the earth, and what will I but that it be enkindled."* "He that would come after Me, let him take up his cross and follow Me;" and sending his Apostles forth into the world, He said to them, "I send you like sheep among wolves."† St. Paul would have all Christians dead and buried with Christ, and, speaking of himself, says that he is crucified to the world, and the world to him, and Holy Writ is full of such sentiments. God has always had, and will have His victims. These were the holy martyrs who shed their blood for His love, the confessors who, dead to themselves, lived and worked for Christ only, and the countless holy virgins who, in the seclusion of their cloisters, lead a life of prayer and self-immolation. Happy

---

* Luke xii. 49. † Luke x. 3.

are those souls who become true victims, consumed by the fire of Christ and seasoned with the salt of His sacrifice.

III. "*I beseech you, therefore, brethren, by the mercy of God, that you present your bodies a living sacrifice, holy, pleasing unto God, your reasonable service.*" * This spirit of sacrifice, so necessary for all Christians, is the groundwork of the devotion which consists in offering our own blood to the Eternal Father, in union with that of His Divine Son, Jesus Christ. If the world can boast of many victims eager to sacrifice themselves for its empty vanities and folly, how earnestly should not the children of light endeavour to follow their crucified Saviour and offer Him all they possess, even their blood and their lives. This is the greatest triumph of grace in the heart of a Christian, implying, as it does, the practice of the most entire mortification and perfect charity. In order to enter upon the practice of this devotion, we should have the following dispositions: First, true *humility of heart*, which will convince us that our offering has no efficacy except through the mercy of God, and that to make it pleasing in His sight we must unite it with the oblation of the Divine Son, Jesus Christ, to His Eternal Father; then will our oblation and offering become but one

---
* Rom. xii. 1.

with that of Christ. Secondly, *sincerity*, which will dispose us to receive from the hands of God any kind of suffering which it may please His Divine Majesty to send us. Without this sincerity we shall be unable to surmount the difficulties we may encounter when called to share the chalice of our Divine Saviour in whatever degree it may please God to make us partakers of it. Lastly, *earnest prayer* is essential, as Our Lord Himself taught us by His prayer in the Garden on the night before His passion. We, too, must beseech the Eternal Father that in so far as He may vouchsafe to accept our oblation He may also grant us strength to accomplish the sacrifice.

The sacred heart of Jesus will be the centre of union for all devout souls who thus dedicate themselves and all they have to the glory of God; this divine heart is the school in which alone can be learnt the science of the saints, for it was here that our divine Master consummated the great sacrifice of Himself, receiving from the hands of His Father the chalice of His passion, and delivering Himself up to death, even the death of the cross.

O my Jesus, I am wholly Thine, and I beseech Thee to accept the offering which I now make to Thee of my blood in union with that most precious Blood which Thou didst shed for me to the last drop on the cross. This union alone can give value to my oblation, which is in itself worthless; do thou deign to receive it, and Thy gracious acceptance will be my reward.

I have not yet shed my blood for Thee, dear Jesus, it is true, but I desire to do so, or, at least, I long to have this desire. Would that I could imitate the holy martyrs, who had the grace to die generously for love of Thee! Vouchsafe, O Lord, through that grace which Thou hast merited for us by Thy passion and death, to bless these my desires and make them fruitful in good works.

EJACULATION.—O most blessed Virgin Mary, Mother of love and mercy, who didst stand by Thy beloved Son upon the cross, deign to assist us poor sinners, who desire to make the oblation of our sinful blood through Thy Immaculate hands, so that in union with the precious Blood of Jesus, it may become an acceptable sacrifice in the sight of the divine Majesty. Amen.

Offerings of the Precious Blood of Jesus.

1. Eternal Father, I offer Thee the merits of the most Precious Blood of Jesus, Thy beloved Son and my divine Redeemer, for the propagation and exaltation of my dear Mother, the Holy Church, for the safety and prosperity of her visible head, the holy Roman Pontiff, for the cardinals, bishops, and pastors of souls, and for all the ministers of the sanctuary.

℣. Glory be to the Father, and to the Son, and to the Holy Ghost.

℟. As it was in the beginning, is now, and ever shall be, world without end. Amen.

Blessed and praised for evermore be Jesus, Who has saved us with His Blood.

2. Eternal Father, I offer Thee the merits of the most precious Blood of Jesus, Thy beloved Son and my divine Redeemer, for the peace and concord of Kings and Catholic Princes, for the humiliation of the enemies of the holy faith, and for the happiness of all Christian people.

Glory be to the Father, etc.

Blessed and praised, etc.

3. Eternal Father, I offer Thee the merits of the most precious Blood of Jesus, Thy beloved Son and my divine Redeemer, for the repentance

of unbelievers, the extirpation of all heresies, and the conversion of sinners.

Glory be to the Father, etc.

Blessed and praised, etc.

4. Eternal Father, I offer Thee the precious Blood of Jesus, Thy beloved Son and my divine Redeemer, for all my relations, friends, and enemies, for the poor, the sick, and those in tribulation, and for all those for whom Thou willest I should pray or knowest that I ought to pray.

Glory be to the Father, etc.

Blessed and praised, etc.

5. Eternal Father, I offer Thee the merits of the most precious Blood of Jesus, Thy beloved Son, and my divine Redeemer, for all those who shall this day pass to another life, that Thou mayest deliver them from the pains of hell, and admit them the more readily to the possession of Thy glory.

Glory be to the Father, etc.

Blessed and praised, etc.

6. Eternal Father, I offer Thee the merits of the most precious Blood of Jesus, Thy beloved Son, and my divine Redeemer, for all those who are lovers of this treasure of His Blood, for all those who join with me in adoring and honouring it, and for all those who try to spread the devotion to it.

Glory be to the Father, etc.

Blessed and praised, etc.

7. Eternal Father, I offer Thee the merits of the most precious Blood of Jesus, Thy beloved Son, and my divine Redeemer, for all my wants both spiritual and temporal, for the holy souls in Purgatory, and particularly for those who in lifetime were most devoted to this price of our redemption, and to the sorrows and pains of our dear Mother, the most holy Mary.

Glory be the Father, etc.

Blessed and praised, etc.

Blessed and exalted be the Blood of Jesus, now and always and throughout all eternity.

THE END.

Devotional and Ascetical Works,

PUBLISHED BY THE

ART AND BOOK COMPANY,
London and Leamington.

BY JOHN BAPTIST PAGANI.

The Anima Divota, or Devout Soul. A new edition, with a sketch of the Author's Life. 18mo. Cloth, 2s.; white cloth gilt, 2s. 6d.; roan, 4s.; best morocco, 7s.

——A Pocket edition of the same. 32mo. Cloth, 1s.

Devotion to the Most Holy Sacrament. 18mo. 2s.

The Church of the Living God, the Pillar and Ground of Truth. 18mo. Cloth, 2s.

In the form of a dialogue between a Catholic and Protestant, showing the foundation of the Church.

The End of the World; or, the Second Coming of our Lord and Saviour. Cloth, 2s. 6d. *net*.

Part I.—Of the principal events which according to prophecy must precede the second coming of Christ. Part II.—The state of the World at the time of His coming. Part III.—The mode of His coming. Part IV.—The principal events coincident with His coming. Part V.—The principal events which will follow His coming.

The Science of the Saints in Practice. Vol. II.—April, May, June. Vol. III.—July, August, September. Vol. IV.—October, November, December. 2s. each, *net*.

A Catechism of Communion. With devotions. 2d.; cloth gilt, 6d.

BOOKS ON THE BLESSED SACRAMENT.

Nouet (Father) S.J. The Octave of Corpus Christi; or, The Mystical Life of our Lord. Being Discourses and Meditations on the Blessed Sacrament. Post 8vo. 3s.

Avrillon (Fr.) Guide for passing Holily the Day and Octave of Corpus Christi. Royal 32mo. Cloth limp, 6d.

Calvary and the Altar; or, Devotions for the Octave of the Blessed Sacrament, the Forty Hours, and the Days of Perpetual Adoration. By the author of "Reflections and Prayers for Holy Communion." With a Preface by Lady HERBERT. F'cap. 8vo., 355 pages. 3s. 6d.

Love for the Holy Eucharist. From the French of the Abbé PETIT. By JAMES MARSHALL, M.A. Post 12mo. 1s.

"There is a freshness of treatment, and an abundance of Scriptural and Catholic, yet simple, instruction in this little volume, which encourages the translator in hoping that to the young especially it will be welcome, both as a preface to their first Communion, and subsequently as a companion to the Altar."—*Preface.*

Hours before the Altar; or, Meditations on the Holy Eucharist. By Abbé de la BOUILLERIE. Royal 32mo. Cloth, 1s.

Baker (Rev. P.) *O.S.F.* The Devout Communicant; or, Pious Meditations and Aspiration for three days before and after receiving the Holy Eucharist. Royal 32mo. Cloth flush, 4d.; cloth gilt, 6d.

Liguori (St. Alphonsus). Visits to the Most Holy Sacraments for every day in the month. With Preparation for and Thanksgiving after Communion. Cloth, 6d.; cloth gilt, 1s.

Confession and Communion Devotions. By the Rev. T. O'HANLON. Cloth, 3s.

The Penitent's Manual, and Fervent Communicant. Cloth, 6d.; roan, 1s.

Communion Prayers for a Week. By Canon ARVISENET. 3d.; cloth, 6d.

ON THE SACRED HEART.

Blessed Margaret Mary Alacoque. The month of the Sacred Heart. Extracted from the Life and Writings of Blessed MARGARET MARY. Translated from the French by the Very Rev. H. B. MACKEY, *O.S.B.* With Preface by the translator. Dedicated to Cardinal MANNING. Post 8vo. 3s.

Month of the Sacred Heart of Jesus. Translated from the French by the Rev. GEORGE TICKELL, *S.J.* Third edition. 6th thousand. Imp. 16mo. 2s.

Huguet (Rev. F.) *Marist.* Month of the Sacred Heart of Jesus. Devotions for every day of the Month, with suitable Prayers, and a method of hearing Mass in honour of the Sacred Heart. Translated from the French by a Sister of Mercy. 3s. 6d.

Ramiere (H.) *S. J.* The Apostleship of Prayer. A Holy League of Christian Hearts united with the Heart of Jesus, to obtain the triumph of the Church and the Salvation of Souls. Translated by a Father of the Society of Jesus. F'cap. 8vo, 388 pp., *reduced to* 3s. 6d.

Lyonnard (J.) *S.J.* Perpetual Intercession to the Agonising Heart of Jesus, for the 80,000 who die every day. 18mo. 1s.

The Life of the Blessed Virgin Mary. With the History of the Devotion to her. From the French of the Abbé ORSINI. To which is added, Meditations on the Litany of the Virgin. By the Abbé BARTHE. Also Poems on the Litany of Loretto. From the German of the Countess HAHN-HAHN. Translated by the Rev. F. C. HUSENBETH, D.D., V.G. With 22 beautiful steel engravings. Imperial 8vo. Published 25s.; reduced to 10s. 6d *net.*

www.ingramcontent.com/pod-product-compliance
Lightning Source LLC
Chambersburg PA
CBHW030307170426
43202CB00009B/909